fishes of western australia

by dr. gerald r. allen

1. *Anampses lennardi.* Lennard's wrasse photographed at Dampier Archipelago, Western Australia.

pacific
marine
fishes

dr. warren e. burgess
&
dr. herbert r. axelrod
editors

book 9

ISBN 0-86622-050-X

Distributed in the UNITED STATES by T.F.H. Publications, Inc., 211 West Sylvania Avenue, Neptune City, NJ 07753; in CANADA by H & L Pet Supplies Inc., 27 Kingston Crescent, Kitchener, Ontario N2B 2T6; Rolf C. Hagen Ltd., 3225 Sartelon Street, Montreal 382 Quebec; in ENGLAND by T.F.H. Publications Limited, 4 Kier Park, Ascot, Berkshire SL5 7DS; in AUSTRALIA AND THE SOUTH PACIFIC by T.F.H. (Australia) Pty. Ltd., Box 149, Brookvale 2100 N.S.W., Australia; in NEW ZEALAND by Ross Haines & Son, Ltd., 18 Monmouth Street, Grey Lynn, Auckland 2 New Zealand; in SINGAPORE AND MALAYSIA by MPH Distributors (S) Pte., Ltd., 601 Sims Drive, # 03/07/21, Singapore 1438; in the PHILIPPINES by Bio-Research, 5 Lippay Street, San Lorenzo Village, Makati Rizal; in SOUTH AFRICA by Multipet Pty. Ltd., 30 Turners Avenue, Durban 4001. Published by T.F.H. Publications Inc. Manufactured in the United States of America by T.F.H. Publications, Inc.

TABLE OF CONTENTS

Editors' Preface

The Fishes of Western Australia departs from our usual format for this series of marine fish books by being authored by someone other than ourselves. It was felt that our friend and colleague, Dr. Gerald R. Allen, Curator of Fishes at the Western Australian Museum, Perth, Australia, could not only supply the excellent photos contained in this book but could also write the most authoritative text for it. Dr. Allen expressed a desire to do the book as it concerned the fauna of his "back yard" so to speak, and it was agreed that he should do it. We are quite happy with the results and are sure that this book comes up to the high standards set by the earlier volumes.

The Fishes of Western Australia covers a group of fishes from an area entirely different from previous volumes so that the overlap of species coverage is minimal. There are also many endemic species that are seen nowhere else in the world. One of the editors (WEB) took a busman's holiday and visited the area this past winter (summer in Western Australia). While snorkeling in the area a number of species depicted in this book were seen "in the flesh," making the editing of this book a more personal venture.

For this volume the physical setup has been changed, with all the color photos being placed together in one section and the text confined to the front. A checklist of the fishes recorded from the area covered is another innovation that should be of great use to people interested in Western Australia.

Dr. Warren E. Burgess
Dr. Herbert R. Axelrod

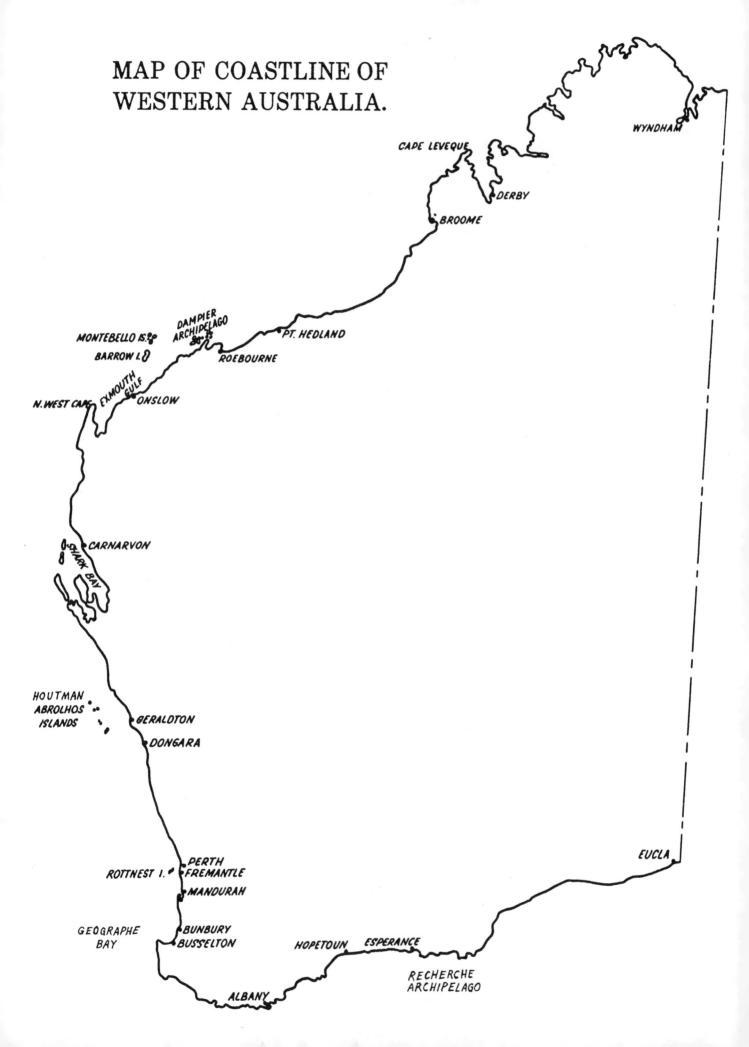

MAP OF COASTLINE OF WESTERN AUSTRALIA.

FISHES OF WESTERN AUSTRALIA

INTRODUCTION

Australia is a land well known for emus, kangaroos, and koalas. The terrestrial fauna contains a wide assortment of unique animals typified by the many marsupial mammals. Although the fact is often overlooked, a large portion of the fish fauna of this island continent is just as unique. When one thinks of Australian fishes attention is immediately focused on the Great Barrier Reef. However, this colossal work of nature, stretching for over 1,900 kilometers (1,200 miles) off eastern Queensland, represents a relatively small portion of the coastline. The fish fauna of Australia actually consists of two very distinct elements, that of the tropical north, containing over 2,000 species, and a much smaller cold-water fauna inhabiting the waters below about 30°S latitude and containing less than 600 inshore forms. Although far from being thoroughly documented, the fishes of the eastern coast are relatively well known, probably because of the presence of the Great Barrier Reef and the fact that the Australian Museum in Sydney has long served as the main center of ichthyological research.

Until recent years the fishes of Western Australia have been largely ignored. This is understandable considering the long distance from Sydney and the fact there has been very little collecting activity even along the populated southwestern portion. Overseas collectors have also bypassed Western Australia, and only a few expeditions have been made there during this century. Consequently the fishes are poorly documented. It will surprise most readers to learn that the coastal fish fauna of Western Australia is possibly the richest on the continent, with approximately 1,539 species recorded to date. The last comprehensive list of the fishes of this region was prepared by the late Gilbert P. Whitley in 1948 and contained only about 740 species. New locality records and undescribed species are presently being compiled at a rapid rate, and the final total will probably approach the 2,000 mark.

Many of the fishes inhabiting the state of Western Australia are found nowhere else in the world. The rate of endemism appears to be about 6.5% or approximately 100 species. However, many Western Australian fishes have distributions that extend only into Northern Territory waters or off South Australia and are therefore unique to the western half of the continent. If these species are also considered the rate of endemism is increased to about 20%. Some of these unique fishes, such as *Pterapogon mirifica, Neatypus obliquus, Anampses lennardi,* and *Coris auricularis,* are among the most beautiful in Australia. In spite of the general figure of 6% there is considerable variation in the rate of endemism among individual families. It ranges from zero in the wide-ranging carangids and scombrids to as high as 41% in the grouper subfamily Anthiinae. Intermediate groups such as damselfishes and wrasses have rates of approximately 10-15%. The 15 largest families in Western Australia in order of abundance are as follows (number of species indicated in parentheses): Gobiidae (90), Labridae (78), Serranidae (61), Carangidae (53), Pomacentridae (52), Apogonidae (51), Syngnathidae (47), Scorpaenidae (45), Monacanthidae (38), Blenniidae (37), Chaetodontidae (28), Clinidae (25), Tetraodontidae (25), Lutjanidae (24), and Carcharhinidae (24). These groups account for 668 species, or about 43% of the total fauna.

The fish fauna of Western Australia is composed of two distinct elements corresponding to geographic regions and their ambient temperature regimes. The fishes of the tropical and subtropical north are by far the largest component with 1,150 species or about 75% of the total fauna. For the most part these are species that have their main distribution north of the latitude of Geraldton and the offshore Houtman Abrolhos. Most of the northern species, particularly those inhabiting coral reef areas, have relatively broad distributions in the Indo-West Pacific. For example, the raccoon butterflyfish (*Chaetodon lunula*) and the scissortail sergeant (*Abudefduf sexfasciatus*) range from the shores of eastern Africa to the islands of the central and southern Pacific.

The other major element is composed of species that live in the cooler, temperate seas along the southern coast and southwestern corner of the state. Most of the 388 species in this category are restricted to the Australia-New Zealand region, although a few are also represented in cool seas of Africa or South America and occasionally in the Northern Hemisphere.

The area between Perth and Shark Bay is a transitional region containing a mixture of tropical and temperate fishes. One of the most interesting localities in this zone is the Houtman Abrolhos, a group of limestone islands supporting rich coral growth and many tropical fishes, but with a significant number of temperate species as well. Approximately one-third (32 species) of the endemic fishes inhabiting Western Australia have their main distribution within this transition zone. They are often the most abundant representatives of their particular family at a given locality.

This volume of *PMF* contains 525 photographs mainly taken in Western Australia during 1974-80 by G.R. Allen and R.C. Steene. Nikon-F cameras were utilized; for underwater photography they were placed in either Ikelite or Hydro-35 housings with electronic flash. Most of the photographs were taken at the following localities under a variety of conditions (usually adverse): Recherche Archipelago, Albany, Cape Naturaliste, Geographe Bay, Rottnest Island, Garden Island, Carnac Island, Houtman Abrolhos, North West Cape, Dampier Archipelago, and the tidal estuary of the Prince Regent River in the Kimberleys.

Occupying about one-third (975,900 square miles) of the total land area of Australia or roughly the entire land mass of the United States west of the Rocky Mountains, Western Australia has an enormous coastline that stretches from Eucla in the southeast corner to the Joseph Bonaparte Gulf in the far north, a distance of 6,960 kilometers (about 4,350 miles). This is a rugged land for the lover of wide open spaces and abundant wildlife. Most of the one million inhabitants of the state are concentrated in the southwestern corner near Perth. The remaining population is widely scattered except for small towns. On northern roads it is not unusual to drive for an entire day without passing another vehicle in either direction. Most of the inland area is comprised of arid desert covered with low scrubby vegetation. This extends to the coast in many places, but it is interrupted in the north by the picturesque sandstone gorges of the Pilbara and Kimberley regions.

The coastal scenery is highly variable. In the south, from Eucla to Cape Naturaliste, the shoreline is extremely rugged and rocky over much of its length. Huge ocean swells, locally called king waves, unleash their fury on precipitous headlands. In certain localities beaches of fine sand, white as snow, form a narrow buffer between the land and ocean depths. The water is extremely clear, but for much of the year it is uncomfortably cold, with temperatures ranging from about 12°C (54°F) in winter to 20°C (68°F) during the southern summer. A good wetsuit is required for extensive underwater work.

From Cape Naturaliste to the Kimberley region the shoreline consists of monotonous stretches of low scrub-covered dunes and sand beaches only occasionally interrupted by steep cliffs and rocky headlands such as those at Kalbarri, just north of Geraldton. North of Onslow there are also vast stretches of mangrove coast, particularly near the mouths of streams and rivers. Between Geraldton and Shark Bay the temperate southern fishes gradually give way to the tropical species that dominate northern waters. However, there is a southerly flowing current system that brings a variety of tropical species to the Houtman Abrolhos and as far south as Rottnest Island, lying 21 kilometers (about 13 miles) off Perth. In the latter area these are particularly evident during the warm summer months. Surprisingly, there are isolated growths of rich coral as far south as the Recherche Archipelago.

From approximately Pt. Quobba, just north of Carnarvon, to the Dampier Archipelago, there is a rich chain of coral reefs extending for some 640 kilometers (about 400 miles). This forms sort of a mini-Barrier Reef and to this day remains little explored by naturalists. Underwater visibility on the northern coral reefs is variable but is generally poor compared with true oceanic reefs. Fifty-foot visibility is generally considered good, but these conditions are rare and underwater photography is often impossible. The turbidity is caused by the nearly continual winds that plague the entire western coast and the large diurnal tides that average between three and five meters. Further north, in the Kimberley region, six- to 10-meter tides are experienced.

Between the Dampier Archipelago and Derby, which forms the gateway to the Kimberley region, the coastal waters consist mainly of extensive sand-bottom areas with few reefs. Mudflats and mangrove swamps are common around Broome and Derby.

The Kimberleys offer some of Australia's finest scenery. Spectacular cliffs of red sandstone plunge into the sea and there are large areas of mangrove growth. Coral reefs are also reported near some of the offlying islands, but conditions for diving and collecting are poor due to greatly reduced visibility and strong tidal currents. Relatively few fishes have been collected in this region because of its inaccessibility.

Aside from the numerous rocky islets along the southern shoreline there are a number of interesting islands along the coast between Perth and the Kimberleys. Above water most of these look alike. . . unimposing desert islands with a thin veneer of low scrub vegetation. Unfortunately there are no lush palm-fringed islands on this coast in spite of the tropical northern latitudes. The islands range in size from several acres (for example Kendrew Island in the Dampier Archipelago) to about 32 kilometers (20 miles) in length and 16 kilometers (10 miles) wide at Barrow Island. Perhaps the most interesting of all the islands are those found in the Houtman Abrolhos, which lie roughly between 28° and 29°S latitude about 50-65 kilometers (31-40 miles) off Geraldton. Although occupying a position far to the south of the zone where reef-building corals generally flourish, there are abundant growths of "table-top" and "staghorn" *Acropora* coral interspersed with areas of sargassum weed and other plant growths that are typical of the rocky coasts of the south. Certainly this group of islands must rate as one of the world's southernmost regions of extensive coral reef. The fishes found there are fascinating, representing an unusual blend of tropical and temperate species.

I thank Dr. David Ride, former Director of the Western Australian Museum, and Mr. John Bannister, present Director, and the Board of Trustees of that institution for supporting this work. I also express gratitude to the numerous people who aided in field work or contributed photographs. These include Mr. Pat Baker, Dr. Paddy Berry, Mr. Norrie Cross, Mr. Andy Chapman, Mr. Jeremy Green, Mr. Barry Hutchins, Mrs. Louisette Marsh, Mr. Nick Sinclair, and Mrs. Shirley Slack-Smith, all of the Western Australian Museum; also Mr. John Braun (Perth), Eve and Bill Curry (Dampier), Mr. Rudie Kuiter (Sydney), Mr. Neil Sarti (Perth), Mr. Ono Sumadhiharga (Jakarta, Indonesia), the late Mr. Arthur Wilson (Dunsborough), and Dr. Barry Wilson (Melbourne). I am also grateful to several ichthyologists who assisted my investigations of Western Australian fishes. Their names, institutions, and groups of specialization are as follows: Dr. J. Bass, Western Australian Museum (sharks); Mr. C.E. Dawson, Gulf Coast Research Laboratory (Syngnathidae); Dr. D. Hoese, Australian Museum, Sydney (Clinidae and Gobiidae); Mr. B. Hutchins, Western Australian Museum, Perth (Batrachoididae, Gobiesocidae, and Monacanthidae); Mrs. S. Jewett, Smithsonian Institution, Washington, D.C. (Gobiidae); Dr. L. Knapp, Smithsonian Institution, Washington, D.C. (Platycephalidae); Mrs. H. Larson, Northern Territory Museum, Darwin (Gobiidae); Mr. R. McKay, Queensland Museum, Brisbane (Sillaginidae); Dr. J. Nelson, University of Alberta, Canada (Creediidae); Dr. J. Randall, Bernice P. Bishop Museum, Honolulu (Labridae); Dr. B. Russell, Northern Territory Museum, Darwin (Labridae and Nemipteridae); Dr. V. Springer, Smithsonian Institution, Washington, D.C. (Bleniidae); Dr. P. Whitehead (Clupeidae and Engraulidae). In addition, Dr. J. Paxton, Curator of Fishes at the Australian Museum, Sydney, kindly provided loans of valuable specimens. Special thanks are due to my wife, Connie, who prepared the typescript.

This volume includes most of the common inshore fishes of Western Australia, illustrating over 400 species belonging to about 90 families. For scientists I have included a comprehensive checklist of the fishes presently known from coastal waters of Western Australia in the Appendix. This contains 1,538 species, including many new records for Western Australia. Most of the species are represented by specimens in the Western Australian Museum, Perth. A more detailed, annotated list is currently in preparation and will be published later.

Gerald R. Allen
Perth, Australia
1 July 1984

Class ELASMOBRANCHII

SHARKS AND RAYS

The sharks and rays represent a primitive group that has evolved relatively slowly. They differ from teleosts (or bony fishes) in that they do not possess a bony skeleton. Instead, the hard parts are formed completely of cartilage that sometimes is partially calcified and therefore may resemble bone. In addition, the higher fishes generally have a single gill chamber with one opening or slit on either side of the head; in sharks and rays there is a separate opening for each of five (six or seven in a few species) gills. The skin is also distinctive and does not contain ordinary scales, but rather a covering of small rough denticles. In some species these are lacking and the skin is smooth.

The sharks form an important segment of the Western Australian fish fauna, with approximately 70 species recorded from there. These belong to 18 families and range in size from the diminutive dogfish sharks (under 300 cm in length) to the gargantuan whale shark and basking shark (both reaching 1200-1500 cm maximum length).

The catsharks and wobbegongs (family Orectolobidae) constitute the second largest group of sharks in Western Australia and are among the most interesting. Many of the species exhibit highly ornate color patterns and a few have decorative tassels (actually flaps of skin on the head or at least around the mouth). The speckled catshark (*Hemiscyllium trispeculare*) is a common inhabitant on coral reefs and is probably nocturnal. During the day it is frequently encountered resting motionless on the bottom in small caves or under "leaves" of tabular *Acropora* coral. Wobbegongs are also common, both on northern and southern reefs. In the former region the tasselled wobbegong (*Eucrossorhinus ogilbyi*) and northern wobbegong (*Orectolobus wardi*) occur. These two are easily separated by the lack of numerous tassles around the mouth in the latter species, which just has a few unbranched tentacles. The Gulf wobbegong (*Orectolobus halei*) of southern waters is generally found resting among weeds or under ledges. All the species in this family are normally non-aggressive, but attacks on humans sometimes occur if the sharks are molested, either intentionally or by accident. I was bitten on the kneecap by a Gulf wobbegong while photographing a pufferfish at Geographe Bay. The shark's head was accidentally knelt on while I was concentrating on the photographic subject in the camera's viewfinder. Luckily the teeth of this small (approximately 60 cm total length) shark failed to penetrate the thick rubber diving suit. Others have not been so lucky; there are reported cases of severe wounds and amputated feet by large wobbegongs (some species reach over 200 cm in length) that were accidentally trod on.

The most publicized Western Australian shark is the great white (*Carcharodon carcharias*) or, as it is locally known, the white pointer. This is perhaps the most ferocious animal in the sea and poses a definite threat to anyone who swims there. Fortunately this species appears to be rare along most of the coast, at least north of Cape Naturaliste. It is most frequently encountered along the southern coast, particularly near Albany, the location of Australia's last whaling operation. The station was finally closed in 1978 because of increased concern over the diminishing whale stocks. During the station's peak of activity approximately 1,000 sperm whales were captured during the annual nine-month season. Attracted to the catch, schools of great whites regularly followed the boats into the whaling station and could be seen swimming around the large buoy where the whales were tied off until processed several hours later. When the whales were butchered the adjacent waters literally turned red, which of course served as an additional attractant to any sharks in the vicinity. It is easy to understand why swimming was strictly forbidden on nearby beaches.

SHARKS OF WESTERN AUSTRALIA

WHITE POINTER SHARK

Carcharodon carcharias

GREY NURSE SHARK

Odontaspis taurus

TIGER SHARK

Galeocerdo cuvieri

WHITE TIP SHARK

Triaenodon obesus

LEMON SHARK

Negaprion acutidens

HAMMERHEAD SHARK

Sphyrna zygaena

S. lewini

S. zygaena

(from Bass, D'Aubrey and Kistnasamy, 1975)

WHALER SHARKS *(Carcharhinus)*

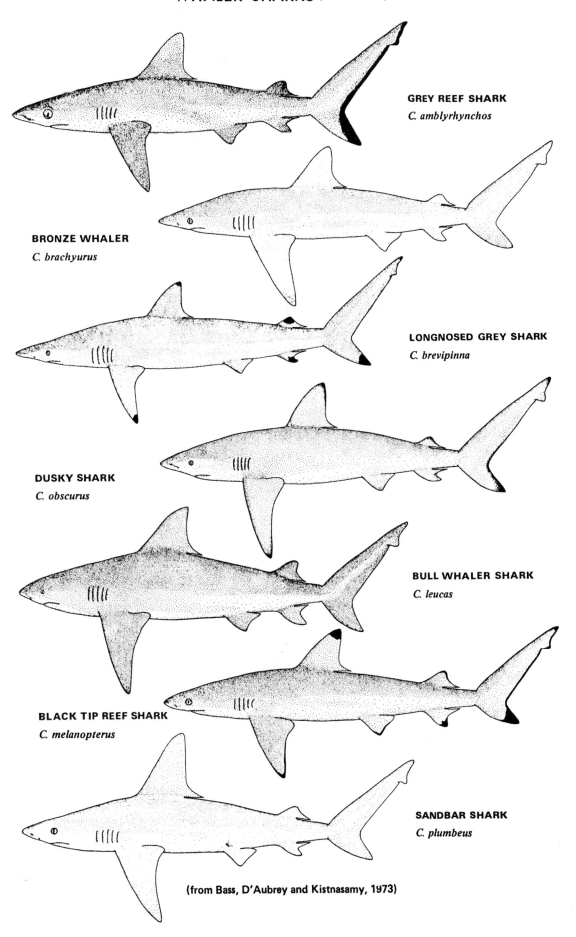

GREY REEF SHARK

C. amblyrhynchos

BRONZE WHALER

C. brachyurus

LONGNOSED GREY SHARK

C. brevipinna

DUSKY SHARK

C. obscurus

BULL WHALER SHARK

C. leucas

BLACK TIP REEF SHARK

C. melanopterus

SANDBAR SHARK

C. plumbeus

(from Bass, D'Aubrey and Kistnasamy, 1973)

The largest great white caught in Western Australia was approximately 550 cm in length (about 18 feet) and weighed about 1,452 kg (3,200 lbs). Sightings of 600-750 cm individuals in the Albany area have been reported in local newspapers but have so far not been substantiated. The maximum size for the species has often been quoted as 35-45 feet, but this figure most certainly represents a gross exaggeration. An article by Dr. John Randall appearing in *Science* reported that the largest officially recorded to date was a 630 cm (about 21 feet) specimen from Cuba.

There are 37 species of rays presently known from Western Australia. The rays are morphologically similar to sharks, but important differences include the enlarged, flattened pectoral fins and ventral position of the gill slits. As with sharks there is a tremendous diversity of shapes and sizes. The manta ray (*Manta birostris*) is by far the largest member of the group, attaining a disc width of over 450 cm. It is an inhabitant of tropical waters and sometimes appears in small groups that visit coral reef areas. These awesome planktonic feeders have a gentle disposition and are easily approached by a diver.

Members of the family Dasyatidae are commonly called stingrays because of the venomous spike that is present on the basal portion of the tail. There are seven species known from Western Australia. The large smooth stingray (*Dasyatis brevicaudata*) is common in cool, temperate waters where it feeds on a variety of fishes, squid, and crustaceans. It grows to over 280 cm in width. Perhaps the most common species in northern Western Australia is the blue-spotted ray (*Amphotistius kuhlii*), a kite-shaped fish with bright blue spots covering the dorsal surface. They are frequently seen resting in holes of the coral reef. The maximum disc width for this species is under 50 cm.

Order ANGUILLIFORMES

EELS

The several families included in this group are distinguished by their very elongate, snake-like body shape with numerous vertebrae. Scales are absent, and most species have a slimy external coating of mucus that facilitates movement through narrow crevices of the reef or in sandy burrows. The paired fins are missing in the majority of species although conger eels, freshwater eels (which spawn in the sea), and some snake eels possess pectoral fins.

Forty-eight species of eels belonging to five families are presently known from Western Australia. Most of the species are either morays (family Muraenidae) or snake eels (family Ophichthidae). The 22 species of morays are mainly inhabitants of northern coral reefs, but at least two, *Gymnothorax woodwardi* and *G. prasinus,* are found in the vicinity of Perth. Most of the species are equipped with sharp, needle-like teeth, and large morays in particular can inflict a nasty wound if provoked by a diver. However, under normal circumstances morays are not aggressive and stories about eel attacks are frequently without a factual basis or exaggerated. All the species are carnivores feeding on a variety of invertebrates and small fishes. The starry eel (*Echidna nebulosa*) has unusual granular teeth that it apparently uses to crush crabs and shrimps that it captures on shallow reef flats. It is one of the more beautiful species and an outstanding aquarium attraction. Perhaps the most common moray on northern reefs is the freckled eel (*Gymnothorax thrysoideus*). This small (length about 60 cm) species is easily recognized by its pale, whitish head.

There are 21 species of snake eels recorded from Western Australia, but further collecting, particularly in northern waters, is bound to produce more. Very little collecting has been done in the open, sandy habitat normally frequented by these eels. They live in sandy burrows and feed mainly on small invertebrates. Many of the species have a hard bony tip at the end of the tail that is used for backwards burrowing.

Conger eels (family Congridae) reside on both southern and northern reefs and exhibit habits similar to those of moray eels. Any gray-colored eels with pectoral fins found in rocky reef areas are likely to belong in this group. The common representative of the family in temperate waters is the southern conger (*Conger wilsoni*) that reaches a maximum length of about 180 cm. In the north this species is replaced by the ashen conger (*Conger cinereus*), a slightly smaller species that attains a total length of about 100 cm.

Order CLUPEIFORMES

BAITFISHES

This group includes primitive herring-type fishes that are generally silvery in color and have a single dorsal fin. The fins contain only soft rays. Most of the Western Australian representatives are relatively small, usually under 20 cm total length. They occur in schools that frequently include several

thousand individuals. Some of the species such as the sprats (*Spratelloides*) are common in coral reef areas; others, like Hamilton's anchovy (*Thryssa hamiltoni*) prefer brackish estuaries and the lower reaches of freshwater streams. Most species feed on tiny planktonic animals and they themselves provide an important source of food for larger predators such as tunas, jacks, and a multitude of sea birds. They also represent an important source of live bait for the tuna industry. Thirty-four species belonging to three families (Chirocentridae, Clupeidae, and Engraulidae) are known from Western Australia.

Families SYNODONTIDAE and AULOPIDAE

LIZARDFISHES

The lizardfishes are a group of relatively small carnivores with ferocious needle-like teeth. They commonly remain motionless on the bottom, poised for action like a miniature rocket on a launching pad. When suitable prey pass by they dash out, seizing the item (usually a small fish) with remarkable rapidity. They are sometimes a nuisance, interfering with the collection of scien-

Synodus sageneus Waite (family Synodontidae). From Waite, 1905. *Rec. Aust. Mus.,* 6(2): Pl. 8, Fig. 1.

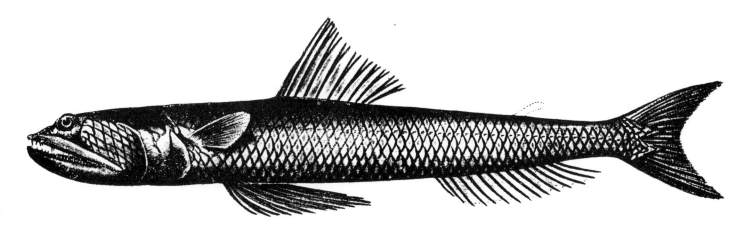

tific specimens by attacking fishes that have been impaled on the collecting spear or by snapping up specimens that have been stunned from the effect of chemicals. Certainly a few potential new species have been lost to science because of their voracious appetites.

The lizardfishes of Western Australia are mainly tropical, and several of the species range widely in the Indo-Pacific region. Most inhabit coral reefs, although the circumtropical *Trachinocephalus myops* is commonly taken by trawl in sandy areas.

The slender lizardfish (*Saurida gracilis*) is the most common species encountered on the reef and ranges as far south as the Houtman Abrolhos, where it is relatively common. This species attains a maximum length of about 30 cm and is found down to a depth of 60 meters.

The sergeant baker (*Aulopus purpurissatus*) is the sole representative of the family Aulopidae. It is a common inhabitant of temperate zone rocky reefs across the southern portion of Australia.

Family CHANIDAE

MILKFISH

This family contains a single species that ranges widely in the tropical Indo-Pacific. It is somewhat herring-like in appearance with silvery coloration and a prominent forked tail. The usual habitat consists of sandy bays, mangrove coast, and brackish estuaries. Occasionally the milkfish penetrates the lower reaches of freshwater streams. Although very bony, the flesh is excellent eating. Milkfish are sometimes cultured in ponds in Southeast Asia and will grow very rapidly if adequate vegetable matter is available for food. The maximum size is about 120 cm total length.

Families ARIIDAE and PLOTOSIDAE

MARINE CATFISHES

There are two families of marine catfishes inhabiting the seas of Western Australia. They can be readily separated on the basis of tail shape. The fork-tail catfishes (family Ariidae) possess a more normal fish-type tail that, as the common name suggests, is strongly forked. The plotosid catfishes, on the other hand, have an eel-like tail gradually tapering to the end. Both groups are characterized by the elongate barbels or feelers around the mouth. These are used for probing in soft mud or sand while searching for food.

The five species of fork-tail catfishes found in Western Australia are very similar in appearance and are difficult to separate. One of the most common is the Australian fork-tail (*Arius graeffei*), which prefers brackish northern estuaries. It also penetrates freshwater streams and it is not unusual to find them many miles upstream in pure fresh water. They readily take a baited hook and the flesh is good eating.

There are eight plotosid catfishes recorded from Western Australia. The striped catfish (*Plotosus lineatus*) is the most abundant species in the tropics, ranging as far south as the Houtman Abrolhos. This fish, which reaches a maximum length of about 90 cm, is frequently encountered in the vicinity of coral reefs, although the large adults are seldom seen. Juveniles form dense schools, sometimes consisting of several hundred individuals, that roam widely over the reef, stirring up areas of soft bottom in search of food (burrowing worms, gastropods, etc.).

The white-lipped catfish (*Paraplotosus albilabrus*) is a solitary dweller that is occasionally seen resting in holes or under the "leaves" of *Acropora* coral. It is almost always inactive during the day and is therefore probably a nocturnal or crepuscular feeder. This species is reported to grow to 120 cm total length, but individuals larger than 40-50 cm are seldom encountered.

Another solitary species that is common on northern reefs is the black-sailfin catfish (*Paraplotosus* species). It was discovered only recently and still remains to be described. Large individuals are solid jet black, but the tiny young exhibit a stunning coloration in which the fins are outlined with a white trim and the barbels are also white.

The common catfish of southern waters is the cobbler (*Cnidoglanis macrocephalus*). There appear to be distinct populations living in marine and estuarine conditions with very little interbreeding between the two. The marine fish are solitary in habit whereas estuarine fish tend to form aggregations and are utilized by commercial fishermen for part of the year. Much of the fish sold in "fish and chips" establishments is cobbler. They attain a maximum length of about 90 cm.

Family BATRACHOIDIDAE

TOADFISHES

The toadfishes (often called frogfishes in Australia) are relatively small, robust animals that vaguely resemble some of the members of the scorpionfish family (Scorpaenidae). They possess strong jaws and a large mouth with several bands of cardiform teeth that enable them to crush crustaceans and molluscs. These fishes occur in all tropical seas; in Western Australia there are six species recorded. They are extremely cryptic in both habits and coloration, effectively blending in with their immediate surroundings. These are passive fishes, and most of their time is spent resting on the bottom waiting for passing prey. Some of the species prefer areas of sand or mud bottom, and it is reported they are able to partially "bury in," leaving only the head exposed. It is possible that the filaments and tentacles on the head and particularly those around the mouth

serve as lures in the same manner as those possessed by the anglerfishes (Antennariidae).

Most of the Western Australian species occur in warm northern seas, but the pink-headed toadfish (*Batrachomoesus rubricephalus*) ranges south of Perth and is present along the southern coast. The most common species on shallow northern reefs is the devil toadfish (*Halophryne diemensis*). This fish grows to about 20 cm total length and prefers dark holes and ledges. It is occasionally seen by divers while searching for rock lobsters in this type of habitat.

Family GOBIESOCIDAE

CLINGFISHES

The gobiesocids are diminutive, goby-like fishes that possess a peculiar sucking-disc on the ventral surface just behind the head. The disc is actually a modification of the pelvic fins and enables the fish to adhere to rocks and seaweed. Clingfishes are usually found in shallow inshore areas where wave action is sometimes strong. The adhesive disc allows them to maintain their position on the bottom in spite of rough sea conditions.

Twenty species, including 10 that are undescribed, are presently known from Western Australia. Most of these are from cool southern waters, but the sea urchin clingfish (*Diademichthys lineatus*) is frequently seen on northern coral reefs. The common name is derived from its habit of associating with prickly sea urchins (*Diadema*). It assumes a vertical position among the spines where it is safe from would-be predators. Unlike most members of the family it spends much of the time swimming above the bottom.

The Tasmanian clingfish (*Aspasmogaster tasmaniensis*) is a common inhabitant of the southern coast. It occurs in shallow water where it is usually found clinging to the surface of boulders.

Family ANTENNARIIDAE

ANGLERFISHES

The anglerfishes or frogfishes are certainly some of the sea's strangest creatures. The first dorsal spine is modified into a slender rod (illicium) that bears a filamentous "bait" (esca) at its tip. This is used to lure small fishes into the vicinity of the cavernous mouth. The prey is then swallowed whole instantaneously. Frogfishes are extremely sluggish, sometimes remaining in the same position for hours while waiting for an unsuspecting victim. The globular body shape and cryptic coloration allow these fishes to blend in extremely well with their surroundings.

There are 17 species recorded from Western Australia. Perhaps the most interesting of these is the spot-tail angler (*Lophiocharon trisignatus*), which occurs along the coast north of Perth. This species has been successfully bred in captivity by local aquarists. A mass of relatively large eggs is attached to the side of one of the parents, where they remain until hatching about two weeks later. The freshly hatched young resemble miniature adults complete with tiny fishing rods that they wave frantically at passing brine shrimp.

The yellow frogfish (*Antennarius nummifer*) is occasionally collected on coral reefs north of Carnarvon. It lives in dark crevices and sometimes assumes the same coloration as surrounding sponges. Specimens larger than about 7 cm are rare.

Order GADIFORMES

COD-LIKE FISHES

This group is represented by four families in Western Australia, the pearlfishes (Carapidae), the codfishes (Moridae), and the cusk-eels (Bythitidae and Ophidiidae).

These are bottom-dwelling fishes that are usually gray or brown in color with slender, tapering bodies. Many of the species possess barbels on the chin. They lead a cryptic existence, sheltering in caves and smaller holes in the reef.

The two common types of codfishes in Western Australia are equally abundant and both are restricted to southern waters. The beardies (*Lotella*) differ from the bearded rock cods (*Pseudophycis*) by having about half as many rays in the first dorsal fin (*Lotella* has five rays). They grow to a length of about 50 cm.

The cusk-eels are represented by 12 species in Western Australia. Several of these are inhabitants of tropical reefs. The pygmy cusk-eel (*Ogilbia* species) is a tiny, 8 cm fish that exhibits a wide variety of coloration including orange, red, pink, brown, tan, and yellow. Unlike most reef fishes that are egglayers, it bears live young that are 2-3 cm in length.

The barbelled cusk-eel (*Brotula multibarbata*) is also found on northern reefs. It has an eel-like shape with continuous dorsal and anal fins. The scientific name, *multibarbata*, is derived from the characteristic cluster of barbels around the mouth. This species grows to a maximum length of about 60 cm.

Orange eelpout (*Dipulus caecus*) is similar in appearance to the pygmy cusk-eel but has sculptured ridges on the snout. It is common along the rocky coast of Rottnest Island, which lies a short distance off Perth.

Family HEMIRAMPHIDAE

HALFBEAKS AND GARFISHES

The halfbeaks are close relatives of the needlefishes and flyingfishes. They are slender, elongate animals with a silvery coloration. The most outstanding feature is the great disparity in size between the elongate lower jaw and the abbreviated upper jaw. These fishes occur in small to large schools that swim near the surface. Most of the species that have been studied are plant feeders, although worms and small crustaceans are sometimes taken. Some of the species are important as foodfishes and baitfishes in Australia.

There are 11 species recorded from Western Australia. Most of these, except for the Southern Sea garfish (*Hyporhamphus melanochir*) are tropical inhabitants, but several of the species range as far south as Perth. *H. melanochir* attains sexual maturity at a fork length of about 25 cm. Spawning occurs during the warm portion of the year or approximately from October to February. About 1,000 to 3,000 eggs are laid; these have a diameter of 1.5 mm and are equipped with filaments that become attached to aquatic plants. The eggs hatch in about two days and the tiny larvae are planktonic for the first stages of their life cycle.

The black-barred garfish (*Hemiramphus far*) is frequently seen in the vicinity of coral reefs, usually occurring in large shoals. The characteristic series of black blotches on the upper sides provides an easy means of identification.

Family ATHERINIDAE

HARDYHEADS

This is a large family containing small, silvery fishes that sometimes form huge schools on coastal reefs, in sandy areas, and in brackish estuaries. They are utilized as baitfish and form an important source of food for larger predatory fishes and sea birds. Most of the species feed on plankton. The family is equally represented in southern and northern waters, with eight species recorded from Western Australia.

Order BERYCIFORMES

SQUIRRELFISHES AND THEIR ALLIES

Most of the members of this group are inhabitants of the deep sea, but several families contain species that inhabit inshore reefs. The Beryciformes represent a transitional group between the lower bony fishes and the more advanced groups. The lower fishes are characterized by an absence of stiff spines in the fins, and many of the species have the pelvic fins positioned in the abdominal region. The beryciform fishes, on the other hand, possess well developed spines in the anterior portion of the dorsal, anal, and pelvic fins and, like many advanced fishes, have the pelvics in a thoracic position, below and slightly behind the pectoral fins. Many of the species are red in color and frequently have very rough scales. There are four families occurring in Western Australia.

The three species of redfish (family Berycidae) are exclusively inhabitants of southern waters. The most common shallow-water member of the trio is the swallowtail (*Centroberyx lineatus*), which also occurs in South Australia. They form large aggregations, frequently mixing with schools of bullseye fish (family Pempheridae) in rocky reef areas. The species also ranges into deeper water down to at least 150 fathoms.

The pineconefishes (family Monocentridae) are represented by two species in Western Australia. These are strange looking creatures with extremely rough scales and pungent spines. The species are believed to be nocturnal. They possess a small light organ near the mouth that is probably used to attract prey. The position of the light organs is also useful for separating the two species; in the knightfish (*Cleidopus gloriamaris*) they are located on each side of the lower jaw, whereas in the Japanese pineconefish (*Monocentrus japonicus*) they are placed under the lower jaw. The knightfish occurs in the Perth area and ranges northward at least as far as the Houtman Abrolhos. At the latter locality it is encountered on coral reefs, sheltering under the "leaves" of *Acropora* during the day. The maximum size for both species is about 20 cm.

The roughy family (Trachichthyidae) is represented in Western Australia by four species. The common roughy (*Trachichthys australis*) is a handsome fish that dwells in caves during the day and forages on smaller fishes and invertebrates at night. It is distributed along the entire southern coast of Australia from southern Queensland to just north of the Perth area.

The squirrelfishes (family Holocentridae) are perhaps the best known members of the order Beryciformes. There are over 50 species that inhabit tropical and subtropical coral reefs; 15 are recorded from northern Western Australia. Most of the species are bright red with large eyes, reflecting their nocturnal habits. The two principal genera, *Myripristis* and *Sargocentron*, are easily distinguished by the absence of a stout spine on the lower cheek in the former genus. The most common species in Western Australia are the hexagon squirrelfish (*Myripristis hexagonatus*) and the red-lined squirrel (*Sargocentron ruber*).

Family SYNGNATHIDAE

PIPEFISHES AND THEIR ALLIES

This group needs little introduction as the seahorses and their pipefish cousins have long been favorites of aquarists. The members of the family share a common body structure that consists of a series of segmented rings with inconspicuous fins. Seahorses are essentially modified pipefishes that have the head on a plane perpendicular to the body and a highly prehensile tail. Both groups have a small tubular mouth. Another important character is the external brood pouch that, oddly enough, is found on

males. The female deposits the eggs in her mate's pouch where they remain until hatching. The family is well represented in Western Australia, with 47 species recorded.

One of the most attractive of the species occurring in northern waters is Janss' pipefish (*Doryrhamphus janssi*), only recently discovered in the Dampier Archipelago. The only specimen collected was taken from a cave in eight meters depth. As the common name suggests, the mangrove pipefish (*Parasyngnathus argyrostictus*) inhabits mangrove estuaries where it lives among submerged tree roots. Gray's pipefish (*Halicampus grayi*) is an extremely small and fragile species, but is nonetheless very beautiful.

In southern waters pipefishes are common inhabitants of sea grass beds. The most abundant species in the Perth area are the two species of *Stigmatopora*, the peacock pipefish (*S. argus*) and the wide-bodied pipefish (*S. nigra*). The females of the latter species differ from the males by having the body greatly flattened.

There are four species of seahorses known from Western Australia; all belong to the circumglobal genus *Hippocampus*. The western seahorse (*H. angustus*) is the most common species in southern waters and is frequently seen around wharves and jetties or floating among weed and other debris. One of the most attractive species is the spiny seahorse (*H. spinosissimus*), which is characterized by spiny projections along the back between each bony segment. There is also a distinct five-pointed "crown" on the top of the head. It is basically a tropical species but sometimes ranges as far south as Perth. The maximum length is about 8 cm.

Perhaps the strangest of all syngnathids are the weedy sea dragon (*Phyllopteryx taeniolatus*) and leafy sea dragon (*Phycodurus eques*). These fishes, which grow to a length of about 30 cm, possess numerous weed-like or leaf-like appendages that are utilized as camouflage. The basic body shape is similar to that of a seahorse.

The ghost pipefishes (*Solenichthys cyano-*

pterus and *Solenostomus paradoxus*) are closely allied to the Syngnathidae, but actually belong to a separate family, the Solenostomidae. The tubular snout of these fishes is relatively long and laterally compressed. Also, unlike their pipefish relatives they possess two dorsal fins and greatly enlarged pelvic fins that in males serve as a brood pouch. The maximum size is about 12 cm. They inhabit reef areas in northern waters, frequently among weed that is either drifting on the bottom or floating near the surface.

Order SCORPAENIFORMES

SCORPIONFISHES

This is an extremely diverse order of fishes containing several hundred species. All are bottom-dwelling fishes that have a characteristic bony plate or suborbital stay extending from below the eye to the gill cover. Many of the species possess venomous fin spines, and the group includes some of the deadliest creatures known to man. Scorpaeniform fishes are well represented in Western Australia, with eight families containing about 86 species.

The family Scorpacnidae is by far the largest. Most of the 45 species inhabiting Western Australia occur in tropical waters. The butterfly cods or lionfishes (genera *Pterois* and *Dendrochirus*) are among the strangest in appearance, with greatly enlarged pectoral rays that are used in cornering small fishes and crabs. The fin spines of these fishes are highly venomous, although the incidence of human deaths resulting from stings is low. Fortunately, the preferred habitat consists mainly of caves and ledges, usually beyond wading depths, thus reducing the risk to humans. Stings can be effectively treated if immersed immediately in hot water to break down or denature the active protein components of the toxin.

The deadliest of all stinging fishes belong to the scorpionfish subfamily Synanceiinae, commonly known as the stonefishes. The hollow dorsal fin spines each contain a

Aetapcus maculatus (Guenther) (family Pataecidae). From Waite, 1905. *Rec. Aust. Mus.*, 6(2): Pl. 15.

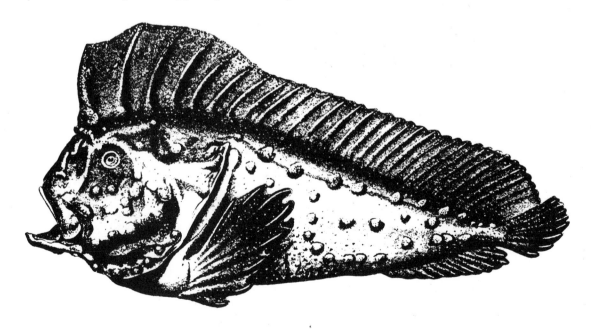

poison gland at the base and when stepped on the victim in hypodermic fashion. There are reported cases of stonefish stingings in which the victims have died within 5-10 minutes. Again, hot water is the best emergency treatment. Unlike the butterfly cods, these fishes pose a definite threat to waders as they are frequently found in shallow water. They have the habit of burying themselves in the sand leaving only the head exposed. Even out in the open they are extremely difficult to detect because of their excellent camouflage coloration and stone-like appearance. There are three stonefish species in Western Australia, the horrible stonefish (*Synanceia horrida*), which grows to about 35 cm, the little stonefish (*Erosa erosa*), and the Dampier stonefish (*Dampierosa daruma*). The last-named species is known only from a few specimens collected between Exmouth Gulf and Broome. The largest of these is about 13 cm in length, which is also the maximum length of *E. erosa*.

The scorpaenid species most often encountered on tropical reefs north of Exmouth Gulf is the northern scorpion (*Scorpaena picta*). It is a secretive fish residing deep in the shadows of holes and crevices. Like many members of the family its coloration is widely variable, ranging from pink or brown to red. One of the rarer species found on the coast is the ornate scorpionfish (*Scorpaenodes varipinnis*). Only one specimen has been taken at North West Cape. It was previously known only from the western Indian Ocean.

Scorpionfishes are also common in the south. Perhaps the most abundant species in shallow coastal and estuarine waters is the devilfish (*Gymnapistes marmoratus*). In deeper offshore areas it is replaced by several larger species including the gurnard scorpion perch (*Neosebastes pandus*) and the western red scorpionfish (*Scorpaena sumptuosa*). Both grow to about 35 cm and inhabit rocky reefs.

The four species that constitute the family known as the prowfishes (Pataecidae) are highly compressed, lack scales, and have a tall continuous dorsal fin. Like most scorpionfishes they are carnivorous and exhibit a cryptic coloration that effectively blends in with the surroundings. They do very little swimming, preferring to remain nearly motionless on the bottom until suitable prey approaches. Two species that are frequently brought into the Western Australian Museum for identification are the red indianfish (*Pataecus fronto*) and the whiskered prowfish (*Neopataecus waterhousii*). The scorpaenid fishes belonging to the genera *Ablabys* and *Paracentropogon* are similar in body shape but frequent northern reefs, whereas the prowfishes are primarily a southern group (*Pataecus fronto* ranges northward to about Shark Bay).

Other scorpionfish families found in Western Australia include the flatheads (Platycephalidae - 17 species), the velvetfishes (Aploactinidae - 11 species), the gurnards (Triglidae - 5 species), the deepsea flatheads (Hoplichthyidae - 1 species), the pigfishes (Congiopodidae - 2 species), and the searobins (Dactylopteridae - 1 species).

Family PEGASIDAE

SEAMOTHS

The pegasids are bizarre looking fishes with a somewhat flattened body, wing-like pectoral fins, and an elongate, tubular snout. They lack scales; instead, the outer body covering consists of a series of hard bony segments. Most of the species are small (under about 12 cm) and are bottom-dwellers that feed on small crustaceans and other benthic invertebrates. The five known species are confined to the Indo-Pacific region. In Western Australia there is only one, *Parapegasus natans*, which is common in the Perth district. Unlike the other members of the family that are mainly marine, this species seems to prefer brackish estuaries or shallow sandy areas such as Cockburn Sound, just south of Fremantle. Seamoths are also captured regularly in the lower reaches of the Swan River.

Families AMBASSIDAE and CENTROPOMIDAE

GLASS PERCHES AND BARRAMUNDI

The Ambassidae contains small, laterally compressed species that are similar to cardinalfishes in appearance and usually silvery or transparent in color. They are primarily inhabitants of brackish mangrove areas and freshwater streams. The Western Australian centropomids, on the other hand, are relatively large serranid-like fishes. The tropical barramundi perch (*Lates calcarifer*) grows to a length of about 180 cm and a weight of over 45 kilos (100 lbs). They inhabit shallow inshore areas, tidal estuaries, and freshwater rivers. The flesh is considered excellent eating and the species is important commercially. The sand bass (*Psammoperca waigiensis*) is similar in appearance but grows to a much smaller size (approximately 40 cm) and is confined mainly to coral reef areas and weed flats.

Family SERRANIDAE

GROUPERS

The groupers (spelled gropers in Australia) are popular with anglers, spearfishermen, and aquarists. The more than 400 species exhibit a wide variety of sizes and shapes. Most are predatory fishes with small scales, a large mouth, and a characteristic "sea-bass" body shape. The serranids and the following orders and families that appear in this book are regarded by ichthyologists as advanced teleosts or higher bony fishes. Most of the groups are members of the Perciformes; the groupers are considered to be very generalized members of this large order, lacking the various specializations found in other families.

The majority of the 60 species occurring in Western Australia inhabit tropical reefs and are of the "sea-bass" type. The world's largest perciform fish, the giant grouper (*Promicrops lanceolatus*), is one of these. Occasional individuals in the 180-220 cm (approximately 6-7 feet) range are encountered in the Houtman Abrolhos and Dampier Archipelago. Specimens exceeding 450 kilos (1,000 pounds) are known from other regions. The large adults are a drab brown or gray color, but juveniles under about 40 cm exhibit a spectacular pattern consisting of white bars and blotches on a black background. The fins are yellow with black spots.

The barramundi cod or polka dot grouper (*Cromileptes altivelis*) is an attractive and highly personable aquarium prize distributed throughout the Indo-Australian Archipelago. In most localities the young are uniformly white or gray with the characteristic pattern of black polka dots. However, on Western Australian coral reefs an unusual variety occurs that has a bright yellow margin on the median fins.

The subfamily Anthiinae contains well over 100 species that inhabit all tropical and warm temperate seas. The group is well represented in Western Australia with 21 species belonging to 12 genera. Many of the species, particularly members of the tropical genus *Anthias,* have a slender body shape and decorative color patterns consisting largely of brilliant shades of pink, red, and yellow. They form large aggregations that feed on zooplankton high above the bottom.

The best known grouper in southern waters is the popular harlequinfish (*Othos dentex*), which exhibits a stunning pattern of large blue spots on a background of bright orange. It frequents rocky reefs down to a depth of at least 40 meters. The breaksea cod (*Epinephelides armatus*) is another common species in the south around rocky areas. It is a curious fish that will frequently approach divers for an inspection at close quarters. The sudden appearance of one of these in front of your face mask in the back of a dark cave can be an unsettling experience. The genus *Ellerkeldia* contains eight species that are distributed mainly in southeastern Australia and New Zealand. Two are known from Western Australia, Wilson's seaperch (*E. wilsoni*) and the red seaperch (*E. rubra*). These fishes inhabit rocky reefs and sponge beds at depths ranging from a few meters to at least 150 meters.

Families ACANTHOCLINIDAE, GRAMMISTIDAE, PLESIOPIDAE, PSEUDOCHROMIDAE, and PSEUDOGRAMMIDAE

DEVILFISHES AND THEIR ALLIES

Under this grouping we have fishes that are closely related to the serranids, having originated from a grouper-like ancestor. Most are very small bottom-dwelling forms seldom exceeding 15 cm in length. The majority of the Western Australian species are inhabitants of holes and crevices in the reef. The soapfishes (family Grammistidae) derive their common name from their soapy mucous coat. This slimy substance has toxic properties and a characteristic bitter taste. The golden lined grouper (*Grammistes sexlineatus*) is the best known member of the family. It is a popular aquarium species that grows rapidly in captivity. Rainford's perch (*Rainfordia opercularis*) is an unusual soapfish with a flattened head and bold color pattern of red and blue stripes. They live in caves and are seldom seen.

The devilfishes (family Plesiopidae) are represented in Western Australia by six species; all except the northern devilfish (*Plesiops coeruleolineatus*) and the spotted devilfish (*Calloplesiops altivelis*) are inhabitants of cool seas. The blue devil (*Paraplesiops meleagris*) is the largest and most striking in appearance, reaching a maximum length of about 40 cm. The two remaining species belong to the genus *Trachinops,* commonly known as hulafishes, that, although placed in the plesiopid family, are unusual in appearance and perhaps merit separate family distinction. Both species, *T. noarlungae* and *T. brauni,* were only recently discovered in Western Australia.

The dottybacks or pygmy groupers (family Pseudochromidae) are coral reef inhabitants with nine species represented in Western Australian waters. The taxonomy of the group is in need of revision and the names used here should only be regarded as tentative. The most conspicuous member of the family is the lined cichlops (*Labracinus lineatus*). This species attains a length of about 25 cm and is abundant on most reefs. It prefers the shelter of caves and crevices but periodically swims out in the open. It is usually unafraid of divers in spite of its relatively small size. Other common species include the various *Pseudochromis* species, especially *P. fuscus.*

Family GLAUCOSOMIDAE

JEWFISHES

This small family is confined mainly to a relatively narrow belt extending from Japan to Australia. Three species are known from Western Australia, and of these the West Australian jewfish (*Glaucosoma hebraicum*) is by far the best known. It is much sought after by anglers and divers because of its excellent table qualities. Adults grow to over one meter in length and a weight of about 25 kilos (55 pounds).

Family TERAPONIDAE

GRUNTER PERCHES

The teraponids are basically a freshwater and estuarine group of fishes that are largely confined to the Australia-New Guinea region. They are laterally compressed and small to medium in size with most saltwater species exhibiting a pattern of stripes or bars on a lighter ground color. The name "grunter" is derived from the strange noise that some of these fishes make when removed from the water.

The tigerfish (*Terapon jarbua*) is an attractive species that is popular with aquarists. They are frequently found in brackish mangrove areas, forming large schools that apparently scavenge over the bottom. Another common species in both northern and southern waters is the yellowtail perch (*Amniataba caudavittatus*), which is easily identified by the yellow fins and bold black markings on the tail. In southern waters

large schools of striped perch (*Helotes sexlineatus*) are frequently encountered in shallow areas where weed and seagrass abound. It is very similar in appearance to the four lined perch (*Pelates quadrilineatus*), which seems to be primarily a tropical form. The two differ markedly with regard to dentition; each tooth of *H. sexlineatus* has three prongs or lobes while the teeth of *P. quadrilineatus* are conical.

Family APOGONIDAE

CARDINALFISHES

The cardinalfishes are the sixth largest family in Western Australia with 51 species thus far recorded. The group is represented in all tropical seas and is in considerable need of taxonomic revision. Many of the species are based on inadequate descriptions

Pelsarita humeralis Ogilby (family Terapontidae). From Waite, 1905. *Rec. Aust. Mus.*, 6(2): Pl. 9.

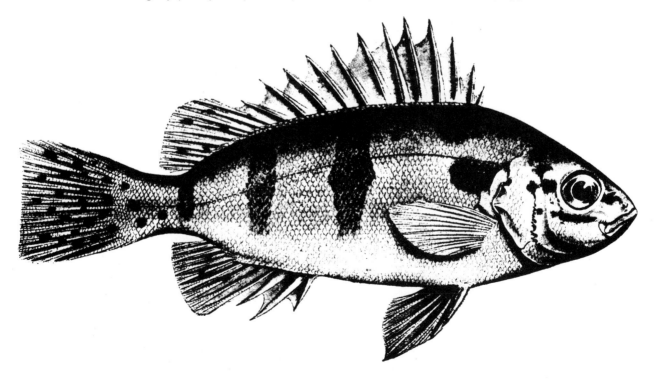

in the literature and a host of others remain undescribed. Generally they are small fishes, usually under about 10 cm in length. Many are red or pink in color and they characteristically possess two dorsal fins, the first usually consisting of six or seven spines. Most of the species inhabit shallow coral reefs and exhibit nocturnal feeding behavior, preferring to remain under cover during the day. The diet consists of small invertebrates and fishes. Cardinalfishes have extremely interesting reproductive habits. An egg mass is deposited by the female and picked up and carried in the mouth of the male. During the incubation period, which varies from a few days to a week or more depending on the species, the egg-brooding male does not feed. On hatching, the larvae, which number from a few hundred to over a thousand, are pelagic for several weeks before assuming the juvenile color pattern and settling on the reef.

Only three species are abundant in cool southern waters. Of these, the gobbleguts (*Apogon ruppelli*) demonstrates a remarkable distribution that extends at least as far south as Cape Naturaliste and ranges northward to Darwin. It is generally found where seagrass and seaweeds dominate the submarine terrain. Another inhabitant of these areas is the southern siphonfish (*Siphamia cephalotes*), which forms transient schools. The remaining member of the trio, the spotted cardinal (*Vincentia punctatus*), frequents rocky reefs where it is a solitary dweller of caves and ledges.

Most of the northern species belong to the genus *Apogon*. These commonly have a pattern of stripes along the sides although a few, such as the two species of red cardinalfish (*A. coccineus* and *A. crassiceps*), are uniformly colored without distinctive markings. The members of the genus *Cheilodipterus* are relatively large cardinalfishes (over 15 cm in length) with big canine teeth in the jaws. The three species of *Rhabdamia* are schooling diurnal fishes that form dense aggregations above the bottom where they feed on plankton. Perhaps the most interesting of

all Western Australian apogonids is the endemic sailfin cardinal (*Pterapogon mirifica*). It is an excessively deep bodied fish with large sail-like dorsal, anal, and pelvic fins. The species attains a maximum length of about 16 cm.

Family SILLAGINIDAE

AUSTRALIAN WHITINGS

The whitings are medium sized, silvery fishes that generally inhabit sandy locales. They have a characteristic conical head and flattened forehead. The mouth is relatively small. The family contains less than 20 species that are confined to the Indo-Pacific region with the strongest representation in Australia. Eight are presently known from Western Australia. In the Perth area, the trumpeter whiting (*Sillago maculata*) is common in shallow water, sometimes travelling in large schools. The various whiting species are popular with anglers and are excellent eating. In some areas they form an important part of the commercial catch. The maximum size is generally between 30-40 cm.

Family POMATOMIDAE

BLUEFISH OR TAILOR

This family is represented by only one species in Western Australia, the popular angling fish known locally as the tailor (*Pomatomus saltatrix*). It is widely distributed in the tropical and temperate waters of the Atlantic, Pacific, and Indian Oceans. Adults attain a maximum length of about 120 cm and have been described as voracious, fast-swimming fish that provide excellent sport for anglers. They are predators that feed in schools, often attacking schools of mullet or other fishes. The name "tailor" is derived from its habit of cutting nets to pieces with its sharp teeth. The annual commercial catch in Australia is in excess of 500 tons, most of which is marketed fresh.

Family CARANGIDAE

JACKS OR TREVALLYS

The trevallys or jacks form a large, circumglobal family with the majority of representatives in tropical and subtropical seas. Most of the species are highly compressed laterally and silvery in color; however, there is tremendous variation in size and shape. Another feature shared by most carangids is a row of scutes or bony plates running along the middle of the tail base.

The family ranks number four in size for Western Australia with 53 species. Several of these are much sought after game fishes such as the yellowtail kingfish (*Seriola lalandi*), which attains a maximum length of about 250 cm and weight of over 330 kilos (150 lbs.). The skipjack trevally (*Pseudocaranx dentex*) is common in southern waters, where it inhabits rocky reefs and sometimes enters estuaries. This species grows to a length of about 75 cm. In the tropics the golden trevally (*Gnathanodon speciosus*) is frequently seen, often in large schools. The flesh of this species is excellent eating, and the fish reach about 100 cm in length. Another common species is the Malabar trevally (*Carangoides malabaricus*), which has an unusually deep body and very large eyes. The black-spotted swallowtail (*Trachinotus bailloni*) is a schooling fish that prefers shallow reefs that are exposed to relatively rough surf conditions.

Several species are characterized by long flowing filaments on the fins. In some, such as the plumed trevally (*Alectis indica*), the filaments are extremely elongate in the young but gradually shorten with increased growth. One of the most striking species is the fringe-finned trevally (*Pantolabus radiatus*), which grows to about 400 cm in length and inhabits northern coastal waters and estuaries.

Family ARRIPIDAE

AUSTRALIAN SALMON

These fishes are not related to the true salmons in spite of their common name. The group contains only two species, the Australian salmon (*Arripis esper*) and the tommy rough (*A. georgianus*). Both are silvery fishes with a single dorsal fin that is prominently notched between the spinous and soft-rayed portions. The Australian salmon is characterized by a rather large size at maturity (approximately one meter total length) and a scale texture that is smooth to the touch. In contrast, the tommy rough reaches a maximum length of only about 40 cm and the body is rough to the touch. These fishes are very abundant along rocky shores in the temperate waters of Australia and New Zealand. They are important commercial species utilized for canning and are taken by netting, purse seining, or trolling.

Families LUTJANIDAE, CAESIONIDAE, CAESIOSCORPIDAE, NEMIPTERIDAE, SPARIDAE, and LETHRINIDAE

SNAPPERS AND THEIR ALLIES

The families in this group contain several species that are important to anglers and commercial fishermen. The largest of these, the true snappers (family Lutjanidae), is comprised of medium-sized fishes frequently exhibiting brilliant coloration. The family is primarily a tropical group that is represented in all warm seas with most species confined to coral reefs of the Indo-Pacific region. There are 24 known from Western Australia. The majority of species belong to the genus *Lutjanus* and are typically "snapper-shaped." They are carnivorous fishes that roam over the coral reef in search of small fishes and various invertebrates. Many of the species are crepuscular feeders, which means they most actively feed at dawn and dusk. The crepuscular feeders frequently form large stationary schools during the day around coral heads or rocky outcrops.

The members of the family Caesionidae are commonly known as fusiliers. Although obviously derived from a snapper-like ancestor, these fishes have forsaken the bottom-dwelling mode of life. Instead the evolutionary pathway has lead them into a planktonic feeding, sardine-like existence. They exhibit a number of modifications that are common among plankton-feeding species belonging to groups that are mainly benthic in habit. These include a very slender body, a forked tail fin, and a small, protrusible mouth equipped with small teeth. These fishes form large colorful schools that swarm above the coral reef. Most of the species are mainly blue in color, frequently with one or more yellow stripes along the sides. Three species are found in Western Australia.

The Chinamanfish (*Symphorus nematophorus*) is a strange snapper that displays a beautiful pattern of blue stripes and has an unusually tall dorsal fin with long trailing filaments. The maximum size of this coral reef dweller is about 90 cm. The flesh is good eating, but in some localities it is avoided because of the danger of fish poisoning (ciguatera).

The butterfishes (genus *Pentapodus*, family Nemipteridae) are similar to the fusiliers in appearance but are bottom-living fishes generally preferring sandy or weedy areas.

The genus is confined to the Indo-Pacific region and is mainly tropical. There are four species recorded from Western Australia. Of these the black stripe butterfish (*Pentapodus vitta*) and ornate butterfish (*P. emeryii*) seem to be the most abundant. The former species ranges far to the south and is common around the Perth district.

The coral breams (genus *Scolopsis*) share several anatomical similarities with the butterfishes, but generally they are deeper bodied and possess several small spines on the suborbital bone (*i.e.,* just below the eye). Five species are presently known from Western Australia, all from tropical waters. The most common are the double lined coral bream (*Scolopsis bilineatus*) and the regal coral bream (*S. monogramma*). These species are found in the vicinity of coral reefs, but like their relatives the butterfishes they prefer open sandy or weedy areas.

The Australian silver breams (family Sparidae) are somewhat snapper-like in appearance but usually are much deeper bodied than the lutjanids and possess peculiar molar-type teeth that are adapted for grinding mollusc shells and other benthic invertebrates. The seven species found in Western Australia form a significant part of the commercial catch, particularly *Chrysophrys auratus*, the flesh of which is commonly billed as "schnapper" at local restaurants and fish shops. The tarwhine (*Rhabdosargus sarba*) is a wide-ranging species found from Japan to South Africa. In Western Australia it is common between Perth and Port Hedland. The maximum size is about 50 cm. The Japanese bream (*Mylio latus*) is a similar sized fish that also ranges widely from Japan to Western Australia and westward to the Persian Gulf.

The emperors (family Lethrinidae) are represented in Western Australia by 10 species. They are conspicuous members of the coral reef community and adjacent sandy areas. They are somewhat similar to silver bream in appearance, but have a characteristic pointed snout.

Family GERRIDAE

MOJARRAS

The mojarras are small silvery fishes that are primarily tropical in distribution, residing mainly in shallow coastal waters and estuaries; some also inhabit the lower reaches of freshwater streams. They are closely related to the slipmouths or ponyfishes (family Leiognathidae). The members of the family are of minor commercial importance although they are sometimes used for bait. Only three species have been found in Western Australia. The silverbelly (*Parequula melbournensis*) is exclusively a temperate species that ranges from Victoria to Western Australia. It is solitary or travels in small schools usually where the bottom consists largely of weed. The maximum size is about 17 cm. In northern waters the flagfin mojarra (*Gerres filamentosus*) is common, particularly around the mouths of streams and in mangrove areas.

Family HAEMULIDAE

SWEETLIPS AND GRUNTS

The sweetlips are medium to large-sized fishes, somewhat snapper-like in appearance, but with pronounced fleshy lips. They are carnivorous, bottom-dwelling animals that live on coral reefs, usually preferring to shelter in caves and crevices. Many of the species exhibit dramatic color changes from the juvenile to adult stages. The young are particularly brightly colored and are much in demand as aquarium fish. They are also favorites with anglers as the flesh provides excellent fare.

Eleven species have been recorded from Western Australian waters. The dusky sweetlips (*Plectorhynchus nigrus*) lacks the bright colors of its relatives but is never-

theless an interesting and attractive fish. The juveniles are sometimes seen in very shallow water and at the approach of danger will "freeze" momentarily, flat against the bottom, drifting to and fro with the waves. They bear a strong resemblance to dead leaves or other debris and in this respect their mimicry is similar to that exhibited by the batfish *Platax orbicularis*. The adults of the pale sweetlips (*Plectorhynchus pictus*) are plain grayish, rather drab fish, but the juveniles are very colorful and highly prized by aquarists. The head is bright yellow and the body is marked with alternating black and white longitudinal bands.

Family MULLIDAE

GOATFISHES

The goatfishes are primarily inhabitants of tropical seas and occur in both the Atlantic and Indo-Pacific. They are small to medium sized fishes with a relatively slender body shape and two separate dorsal fins. The name "goatfish" is derived from the pair of prominent "whiskers" or barbels on the chin. Apparently the barbels are equipped with specialized cells that act as taste buds. These are used for probing the sandy bottom in search of food, consisting mainly of benthic invertebrates. Preferred items include polychaete worms, shrimp, and brittle stars. Many of the species are brightly colored with various shades of yellow and red.

Seventeen species are known from Western Australia. All of these are tropical except the blue-spotted goatfish (*Upeneichthys lineatus*), which occurs along the entire south coast and ranges northward to about Shark Bay. On northern reefs the blackspot goatfish (*Parupeneus fraterculus*) and the Indian goatfish (*P. indicus*) are perhaps the most common. The former species also occurs outside of the tropics, ranging as far south as the Perth area, where it can be seen at Rottnest Island. Both are frequently found in areas of weed with occasional sand patches.

Family PEMPHERIDAE

SWEEPERS OR BULLSEYES

The pempherids are inhabitants of both northern and southern waters. There are perhaps more species in Australia than any other locality. Most are small, usually under about 20 cm total length. Characteristically these fishes have a flattened dorsal outline with a prominent, rounded ventral outline. They are laterally compressed with a single dorsal fin and are usually brownish in color. Typically they form large aggregations in caves or under ledges during the day, coming out in the open at night to feed. Preferred food items include crabs, shrimp, polychaetes, and small cephalopods.

Eleven species have been recorded from Western Australia. The most common one in cool southern waters is the rough bullseye (*Pempheris klunzingeri*), which, unlike its northern relatives, sometimes forms large diurnal schools that swim up to several meters above the bottom. Several species are abundant in northern waters, but the largest schools are formed by the bullseye sweep (*Parapriacanthus unwini*). Several thousand individuals of this 10 cm fish sometimes flock together in a single cave.

Family TOXOTIDAE

ARCHERFISHES

The archers are relatively small, laterally compressed fishes, usually with a series of black blotches or bars on the upper sides. They are renowned for their ability to knock down insects with a jet of water. The aqueous bullets are produced by suddenly pulling in the gill flaps, forcing out water through a tube formed by a groove on the roof of the mouth. The accuracy of the fishes' aim is amazing considering they must compensate for the angle of refraction of light. Because of the bending of light rays as they enter the water, archerfishes view their targets in positions different from the true ones.

The habitat of archerfishes consists mainly of mangrove-bordered estuaries and the brackish lower reaches of small streams. However, they sometimes penetrate pure fresh water and it is not unusual to find archers more than 150 km from the sea. During the day they continually feed at the surface. Young fish form small aggregations around half-submerged roots, logs, or under overhanging branches. The adults roam considerable distances along the shoreline, rarely venturing out over deep water. Contrary to popular opinion, archers don't obtain all their food by shooting it down. Much of it consists of items already floating on the surface. Mosquitoes and various flies and gnats are eaten in large quantities.

In Western Australia there are two species recorded, both apparently restricted to the Kimberley region. The most common species is the spotted archerfish (*Toxotes chatareus*). Although they usually don't exceed 25 cm in length the flesh is reasonably good eating. It is easy to catch these fishes with a small hook baited with a live grasshopper or large fly.

Family KYPHOSIDAE

SEA CHUBS OR BUFFALO BREAMS

Kyphosids are conspicuous residents of shallow reefs in both temperate and tropical waters. Many of the species are gray in color and all have a relatively small mouth and fine teeth that are used for grazing on algae. The members of the genus *Kyphosus* typically form large schools that frequent rocky reefs adjacent to shore. The flesh is eaten in some localities, but it is not particularly good.

Six species are known from Western Australia. The most strikingly colored is the zebrafish (*Girella zebra*), which occurs south of Geraldton. Specimens from depths greater than about 3-4 meters are boldly marked with alternating black and white bands. Juveniles and individuals living in tide pools and shallow water are usually drab with gray instead of white bars. The members of the genus *Kyphosus* are called rudderfishes or sea chubs in other parts of the world, but in Western Australia they are known as buffalo bream because of their relatively large size (maximum about 75 cm total length) and schooling behavior. The western buffalo bream (*Kyphosus cornelii*) is known only from Western Australia from about Shark Bay to Cape Naturaliste.

Family EPHIPPIDAE

SPADEFISHES

The ephippids are a small family of tropical shore fishes that are generally deep-bodied and strongly compressed laterally. The best known members of this family in the Indo-Pacific region belong to the genus *Platax,* known to aquarists as batfishes. Young batfishes display greatly disproportionate dorsal and anal fins that enhance their overall beauty and graceful swimming behavior. As the fish increases in size the fins become smaller in relation to the body. The maximum size reached by these fishes is about 50 cm total length, and in some parts of Southeast Asia they are utilized as food.

In Western Australia there are five species known; three of these belong to the genus *Platax*. The Batavian batfish (*Platax batavianus*) is common in the Dampier Archipel-

ago. Young fish are encountered sheltering in reef crevices, but large adults swim in the open in small groups or pairs. The nine-spined batfish (*Zabidius novemaculeatus*) is seen less frequently. It greatly resembles a *Platax* but has nine instead of five to seven dorsal spines. The spotted spadefish (*Drepane punctata*) is an inhabitant of mangrove estuaries and the murky coastal waters of the Kimberley region. The flesh of this species, which grows to about 30 cm total length, is good eating and juveniles make handsome aquarium specimens.

Family SCATOPHAGIDAE

SCATS

This small family contains only a few species confined to the tropical Indo-Pacific. They are laterally compressed fishes that greatly resemble the marine butterflyfishes (family Chaetodontidae) in shape. Only two species are known from Western Australia, the spotted scat (*Scatophagus argus*) and the banded scat (*Selenotoca multifasciatus*). Both inhabit mangrove estuaries and the lower reaches of freshwater streams, principally in the Kimberley region. The maximum size attained is approximately 30 cm, but most specimens are considerably smaller. Juveniles are well suited for life in captivity.

Family SCORPIDIDAE

SWEEPS OR FOOTBALLERS

The scorpidids (not to be confused with the scorpaenids or scorpionfishes) are primarily a temperate Australian group, although one species, the stripey (*Microcanthus strigatus*) is also found on rocky coasts of China, Japan, and the Hawaiian Islands.

These fishes are closely related to the colorful butterflyfishes, which are treated next. Both groups contain laterally compressed, deep-bodied species that have a small mouth and fine bristle-like teeth. They are inhabitants of rocky reef areas where heavy growths of seaweed dominate the seascape. Solitary individuals are sometimes encountered, but usually small to large schools are seen. The common name is derived from the striped color pattern exhibited by several of the species that is similar to a pattern commonly seen on Australian football (soccer) jerseys. The species are small (usually under 25 cm) and are unimportant as commercial fishes.

Ten species inhabit temperate Australia, with only the stripey ranging into subtropical Queensland and Western Australia. The distribution of the stripey is an enigma. Isolated pockets or populations are present in Australia, the eastern coast of Asia, and the Hawaiian Islands. In Australia the species is found on the east coast from just south of Sydney to the Capricorn Group off Queensland. It is absent along the entire southern coast but reappears in Western Australia between Cape Leeuwin and Shark Bay. The western population has been described as a separate species, *Microcanthus vittatus,* but the validity is questionable. Stripeys inhabit rock pools and adjacent reefs and on the southern fringes of the tropics are found in live coral areas.

Members of the genus *Scorpis* are referred to as sweeps. Two species are found in Western Australia, the banded sweep (*S. georgianus*), which inhabits rocky shallows, and the sea sweep (*S. aequipinnis),* which is found in deeper offshore waters. The latter species is primarily silvery in color and has much fainter bars than *S. georgianus.*

Of the five species occurring in Western Australia, the most attractive is the western footballer (*Neatypus obliquus*), which is endemic to the state. Emblazoned with six copper-colored bands on a field of white, the footballer forms huge shoals above the bottom. They are enormously curious fishes that will approach a diver at close quarters with a complete lack of fear.

The last Western Australian member of the group, *Tilodon sexfasciatum,* commonly known as the moonlighter, is conspicuously marked with alternating black and white bands. It is an inhabitant of temperate rocky reefs, ranging across southern Australia to New South Wales.

Families CHAETODONTIDAE and POMACANTHIDAE

BUTTERFLYFISHES AND ANGELFISHES

This assemblage is well known to aquarists and coral reef visitors. There are probably no other families of fishes that exhibit such a wide range of exotic color patterns. Many ichthyologists have considered the butterflys and angels as members of the same family, but a study by Dr. Warren E. Burgess indicates there are several good reasons for separating them. These include the prominent cheek spine found only in the angels and the bony plates present only in larval butterflyfishes. Nearly all pomacanthids and most chaetodontids are found on tropical coral reefs; there are, however, a few exceptions living on temperate Australian reefs. These include the truncate coralfish (*Chelmonops truncatus*) and a scattering of tropical forms that occasionally stray as larvae as far south as the Sydney and Perth areas.

Most of the 28 species of butterflyfishes occurring in Western Australia are widespread Indo-Pacific forms that have been illustrated and discussed in previous *PMF* volumes. However, several are deserving of mention. The assarius or western butterfly (*Chaetodon assarius*) is found only in Western Australia, ranging from Exmouth to Perth. It is very similar in appearance to

C. guentheri from the eastern coast of Australia and China and Japan. It is occasionally seen in only 2-3 meters depth, but more often it is encountered in deeper water (over 10 meters). It is very common in the Houtman Abrolhos. The willemawillum or margined coralfish (*Chelmon marginalis*) is abundant north of Carnarvon and occurs along the entire northern coast of Australia to the Cape York Peninsula. South of there, along the Great Barrier Reef, it is replaced by *Chelmon rostratus*. One of the rarest species in the state is the Bantayan butterflyfish (*Chaetodon adiergastos*) which has been sighted only occasionally at North West Cape and the Dampier Archipelago. Only one specimen has been collected.

Eleven species of angelfishes are known from Western Australia. The most common ones seen on coral reefs are the emperor angelfish (*Pomacanthus imperator*) and the semicircle angelfish (*P. semicirculatus*). In deeper water off North West Cape the three-spot angelfish (*Apolemichthys trimaculatus*) is occasionally seen. The two members of the genus *Chaetodontoplus*, the scribbled angelfish (*C. duboulayi*) and the yellowtail angelfish (*C. personifer*), are usually seen either in sandy areas below 3-4 meters depth or in deeper water with a flat hard bottom and a low growth of sponges and gorgonians. Both species were thought to be endemic to northern Australia until they were reported from Taiwan in *PMF* Volume 5 on the basis of photos of preserved specimens taken by Dr. S. Shen. However, it is my belief that these records are erroneous and in all likelihood the specimens originated from Australia. Taiwanese trawlers are frequently apprehended by authorities for illegally fishing in Australian waters. Among the confiscated catches of three boats recently arrested off Western Australia were large numbers of local reef fishes including both species of *Chaetodontoplus*. The fishes were frozen fresh in good condition and normally would be sold on the Taiwan market. Certainly Taiwanese fish

vendors would be the last to admit their "fresh" seafood was from far-away Australia.

The pygmy angels belonging to the genus *Centropyge* appear to be very rare in Western Australia. Only one species, the white spot angel (*C. tibicen*) is relatively common, but it has only been taken in the Houtman Abrolhos and the North West Cape area. Eibl's angel (*C. eibli*) was recently discovered at North West cape and is known only from a few specimens. It also occurs at the Maldive Islands and Indonesia.

Family ENOPLOSIDAE

OLD WIFE

This is strictly an Australian family containing only a single species, *Enoplosus armatus*. The general body shape and markings resemble some of the butterflyfishes, but there are two separate dorsal fins that are triangular in shape and somewhat elongate. The species occurs along the southern coast of Australia from northern New South Wales to about Geraldton, Western Australia. It is an inhabitant of rocky reef areas, frequently seeking shelter among sargassum fronds or under the canopy of these weeds. It feeds on a variety of benthic invertebrates.

Family POMACENTRIDAE

DAMSELFISHES

The pomacentrids are small, reef-dwelling fishes found in all warm seas; a few of the species occur in temperate and subtropical areas. The majority are territorial bottom-dwellers, although some (mainly in the genus *Chromis*) form large mid-water aggregations. The members of the family are too small to be of commercial importance, only occasionally being used for bait. Damselfishes are popular with aquarists because of their bright colors and interesting behavior, although they are not ideally suited for captivity because of their strong territoriality and pugnacious nature. The body shape is variable, ranging from ovate in *Dascyllus* and *Amblyglyphidodon* to elongate in *Lepidozygus* and *Neopomacentrus*. There is a single dorsal fin with a usual compliment of nine to 14 spines and an anal fin with two spines. The various species exhibit a wide variety of dentition. The two basic types are: (1) relatively elongate close-set teeth with flattened tips found in algae-eating fishes such as *Abudefduf,* and (2) stubby conical teeth found in plankton-feeding fishes exemplified by *Chromis*. Most pomacentrids exhibit a stereotyped reproductive pattern in which an elaborate ritual of courtship and nest preparation is followed by intensive parental care during the incubation period. The eggs, which number from a few hundred to several thousand, hatch in two to three days to one week, depending on the species, and the young are pelagic for at least several weeks.

The family ranks fifth is size in Western Australia with 52 species. All except the scalyfins (genus *Parma*) and two *Chromis* are inhabitants of warm tropical waters. The scalyfins are mainly confined to Australia although they are represented by one or two species at New Zealand, Lord Howe Island, Norfolk Island, and New Caledonia. These are relatively large herbivorous pomacentrids inhabiting rocky, weed-covered reefs. The young of most species are bright yellow with blue lines and spots.

Most of the tropical pomacentrids in Western Australia are wide-ranging forms that have been featured in previous *PMF* volumes. However, there are a few exceptions discussed below. The northwest anemonefish (*Amphiprion rubrocinctus*) resembles the popular *A. frenatus* of the Philippines and east coast of Africa. The

range of this species was formerly believed to consist of two elements, one from northwest Australia and another from Fiji, Samoa, and the Society Islands. Recent investigations reveal that the Australian population is distinct and the Pacific fish probably represents an unusual color variety of *A. melanopus*. Miller's damsel (*Pomacentrus milleri*) is another species unique to Australia and ranges from the Northern Territory down the west coast to Perth. It is the only truly tropical pomacentrid that has established a permanent breeding colony at Rottnest Island. The western gregory (*Stegastes obreptus*) was previously known only from Western Australia but was recently collected at Indonesia. It is closely related to *S. apicalis* of the Great Barrier Reef and is perhaps derived from the same ancestral stock.

The genus *Chromis* is the largest in the family, but there are relatively few species represented in Western Australia, probably because of the lack of conditions that typify their preferred outer reef habitat. They normally frequent steep drop-offs where water visibility is generally good. However, the eight species that occur in the state include three that are apparently endemic to Western Australia. One of these, the blackheaded puller (*Chromis klunzingeri*), is confined to southern waters between Geraldton and the Recherche Archipelago.

Order CIRRHITIFORMES

HAWKFISHES AND THEIR ALLIES

The hawkfishes (family Cirrhitidae) and related families were sometimes grouped in a single unit, the Cirrhitiformes, by early authors. Although recent studies have shown the group to be quite divergent and possibly polyphyletic, this lumping is often used for convenience. Basically, the fishes that fall into this category are benthic dwellers of coral reefs and temperate rocky reefs. Many have a hawkfish shape with free projecting rays on the lower part of the pectoral fins that are adapted for perching on the bottom. Characteristically there is a single dorsal fin with 15 or more spines and a prominent notch between the spinous and soft portions.

Hawkfishes are found in all tropical seas, with most occurring in the Indo-Pacific region. The common name is derived from their habit of perching on coral heads, gorgonians, etc., from which they swoop down on passing prey (*i.e.*, fish or small crustaceans). Most of the fishes are small, usually less than 12 cm total length. Seven species have been recorded from Western Australia. They seem to be most abundant around North West Cape and, strangely, are rare at Dampier Archipelago, further to the north. The red barred hawkfish (*Cirrhitichthys aprinus*) ranges as far south as the Houtman Abrolhos. The lyretail hawkfish (*Cyprinocirrhites polyactis*) is known from the state only on the basis of a few specimens collected at a depth of 132 meters.

The members of the family Chironemidae are known as kelpfishes because of their affinity for weedy areas. They are similar to hawkfishes in appearance but strictly temperate in distribution. Of the two species that reside in Western Australia, the most common is the silver spot (*Threpterius maculosus*). The name is derived from the characteristic marking on the posteriormost projection of the gill flap. The species reaches a maximum size of about 30 cm.

The species in the family Aplodactylidae are known as sea carps. The western sea carp is the sole representative in the state and is an inhabitant of temperate seas. This species has a typical notched dorsal fin but lacks the projecting pectoral rays of other "cirrhitiform" fishes. It has unusual trilobate teeth that are used for feeding on algae. Although it reaches a maximum length of over 40 cm, the flesh is considered very poor eating.

The morwongs (family Cheilodactylidae)

are conspicuous residents of southern reefs wherever there is a rocky habitat. Several of the members of this group exhibit strongly contrasted color patterns of black and white, and the juveniles are favorite aquarium attractions. Adults grow to a maximum length of 60 cm or more. Surprisingly, the most common species around Perth, the red lip morwong (*Cheilodactylus rubrolabiatus*) was described just recently. It ranges as far north as the Houtman Abrolhos, where it occurs on coral reefs and in weedy areas. The tiny young (under about 4 cm total length) first appear in shallow rock pools as silvery, free-swimming fish with a sharply compressed breast and abdomen. They quickly assume the characteristic dark bars and settle into a benthic existence. Five other morwong species are found in Western Australia.

Family MUGILIDAE

MULLETS

The mullets are silvery coastal fishes that occur in large schools and are of considerable economic importance. Characteristic features include two widely separated dorsal fins and a small mouth, either without teeth or, if they are present, minute teeth. These fishes are common in brackish estuaries, mangrove swamps, and the lower reaches of freshwater streams. They also inhabit sandy areas adjacent to coral reefs. Seven species are recorded from Western Australia, all except Forster's mullet (*Aldrichetta forsteri*) being inhabitants of the tropics. The last mentioned species is particularly common in southern estuaries. It is easily recognized by the bright yellow eyes. Perhaps the most common of the northern mullets is the diamond scale (*Liza vaigiensis*), which is caught in large quantities by commercial fishermen using seine nets. The flesh is rich, has few bones, and is considered excellent eating. In

Southeast Asia mullets are cultivated in ponds on a large scale.

Family SPHYRAENIDAE

BARRACUDAS

The barracudas are elongate silvery fishes with ferocious teeth. Some species get very large and the flesh is considered good eating. A number of species (and genera) have been listed for Western Australia, but only six of these seem to be reliable. The largest and best known is the great barracuda (*Sphyraena barracuda*), which is found in all warm seas. In the Caribbean it has been implicated in attacks on humans. They are readily attracted to shiny or light-colored objects, and many of the mishaps involving barracudas were caused by the victim dangling feet or arms in murky water, either off piers or from boats. These fish often travel in large schools, thus increasing the danger. Fortunately attacks have very rarely been reported from the Indo-Pacific region. The great barracuda is the largest member of the family, growing to a maximum length of 180 cm. In southern waters the striped seapike (*S. obtusata*) is common around rocky reefs and weedy areas, where it forms huge stationary shoals. The fish is silvery but has a yellow tinge and is much smaller than the great barracuda, growing to only 20 to 30 cm in length.

Family LABRIDAE

WRASSES

This is the second largest family of fishes in Western Australia, with 78 species thus far recorded. Wrasses are always conspicuous at all latitudes in the state and in a variety of habitats ranging from rocky reefs and coral reefs to areas of sand and weed. They are most abundant in shallow water but range down to a depth of at least 50 meters. It is difficult to describe a "typical" wrasse as the group is extremely variable with regard to size and shape. Most are small to medium sized with a laterally compressed body. There is a single dorsal fin that contains eight to 13 relatively feeble spines. Many species are among the most spectacularly colored of all fishes; others are garbed in drab tones of gray and brown. Some exhibit dramatic color changes from the juvenile to adult stage, and sexual dichromatism is common. In most species females possess the ability to transform into the male sex when a certain growth stage is reached or under certain social conditions. The cleaner wrasses (*Labroides*) form territorial aggregations consisting of a "harem" of females and a single dominant male. If the male is killed or experimentally removed, the most aggressive female rapidly changes into the male sex. This type of sex reversal in wrasses is probably more common than was previously believed. In most instances the large colorful adult males (usually referred to as the terminal male phase) are relatively scarce. Color changes of this type have created much confusion with scientific names. In many cases a single species may have a different Latin name for each growth stage or color phase.

In the colder waters of temperate Western Australia several genera are represented. They are frequently referred to by anglers as parrotfishes, a name usually reserved for the tropical Scaridae, which have the teeth fused into a parrot-like beak. Wrasses are easily distinguished from this group on the basis of dentition, which generally consists of separate canine-type teeth with enlarged "tusks" frequently present at the front of the jaws. One of the most abundant of the southern species is the brown-spotted wrasse (*Pseudolabrus parilus*), which has distinct male and female color forms. The genus *Coris* is normally found in tropical waters but is represented by a single abundant species, *C. auricularis*, in southern Western Australia. It is a resident of sandy areas adjacent to weed-covered reefs. It is frequently found in the company of another common southern wrasse known as the Maori (*Ophthalmolepis lineolatus*). Unlike many labrids, species of *Coris* and *Ophthalmolepis* have relatively small scales. Another common inhabitant of southern waters is the black-spotted wrasse (*Austrolabrus maculatus*), which anatomically is closely related to *Pseudolabrus*. It prefers areas of dense weed, but the bright red ground color is rather conspicuous among these surroundings, at least in shallower depths. The largest wrasse in Western Australia is the southern-dwelling blue grouper (*Achoerodus gouldii*), which grows to a total length of over 140 cm. Again, this fish is erroneously named, as "grouper" is commonly used for members of the family Serranidae. It is a favorite food fish in some localities.

There is a bewildering variety of tropical wrasses in Western Australia. Most are small, brightly colored inhabitants of coral reefs. Several are unique to the state and deserve special mention. Lennard's wrasse (*Anampses lennardi*) is unusual in that the female "outshines" the terminal male phase with regard to color pattern. The highly contrasted yellow and sky blue stripes make this one of our most beautiful fishes. It is surprising that this species remained undetected by science until only recently. The seven banded wrasse (*Thalassoma septemfasciata*) also represents a relatively recent discovery. It is found in shallow wave-swept areas from North West Cape to Perth. Two undescribed species of tuskfish (*Choerodon*) are the newest additions to the Western Australian wrasse fauna. The genus *Choerodon* is widely distributed in the Indo-Pacific region, but most species are confined to Australian waters. These are generally deep-bodied wrasses with a blunt head. The common name is derived from the very large teeth at the front of the jaws. These are used for feeding on crabs, molluscs, and small fishes. All wrasses are carnivores, although some algae is occasionally ingested. Some species, such as those belonging to the genus *Cirrhilabrus*, feed on plankton.

Family ODACIDAE

WEED WHITINGS AND TUBEMOUTHS

The family Odacidae is closely related to the wrasses, differing chiefly with regard to dentition. Unlike labrids, which have separate teeth, the weed whitings possess fused teeth that resemble those of parrotfishes, although one species has a supplementary row of canines. The body shape of most species is elongate and the snout is usually pointed. Weed whitings are inhabitants of grass beds and rocky, weed-covered reefs normally in depths less than 10 meters. Most of the species are mottled with various shades of green, brown, and red. They are well camouflaged and difficult to detect amid their weedy surroundings. Most varieties are under 20 cm in length, but the herring cale (*Odax cyanomelas*) grows to over 45 cm. Nine species are known from southern Western Australia.

The rainbowfish (*Odax acroptilus*) ranges from the Houtman Abrolhos southward. It is found among dense weed, only occasionally surfacing above the vegetative canopy. Males are extremely bright-colored and possess several elongate spines anteriorly on the dorsal fin. The species attains a maximum length of about 20 cm.

The tubemouth (*Siphonognathus argyrophanes*) is an extremely elongate fish that lacks pelvic fins and superficially resembles the cornetfishes (family Fistularidae). The maximum size is about 45 cm.

Family SCARIDAE

PARROTFISHES

Scarids are schooling herbivorous fishes that are mainly confined to tropical coral reefs. The general morphology is similar to that of the labrids, but they tend to be larger and exhibit teeth that are fused into beak-like plates. This serves as an efficient mechanism for grazing on the fine mat of algae that covers dead coral reefs. A considerable amount of calcareous material is ingested along with the algae and is crushed into a fine powder by the specialized pharyngeal teeth. This fine sediment is eventually evacuated with the feces and accounts for a significant portion of the sediment found in coral reef areas.

The parrotfishes of Western Australia are poorly documented. At this writing there are 14 species known from the state, but this total is certain to increase. Scarids exhibit the same sort of color changes and sex reversal previously discussed for the wrasses, and this has resulted in a great deal of nomenclatural instability. Parrotfishes are generally abundant on coral reefs of the Houtman Abrolhos and northward. A few of the tropical species, including *Leptoscarus vaigiensis*, *Scarus ghobban*, and *S. sordidus*, are year-round residents at Rottnest Island off Perth.

Family OPISTOGNATHIDAE

JAWFISHES

The jawfishes or monkeyfishes are peculiar creatures with an elongate blenny-like body and a greatly oversized head. The cavernous mouth, equipped with numerous teeth, is used for feeding on a variety of items that include small fishes and crusta-ceans. It is also a reproductive adaptation utilized for oral egg incubation. Behaviorly these are highly interesting fishes that construct elaborate pebble-lined burrows in sand and fine rubble. They are apparently territorial, but the burrows tend to be widely spaced. Of the four species occurring in Western Australia, the Darwin jawfish (*Opistognathus darwiniensis*) is the most brightly colored. The maximum size is approximately 40 cm total length.

Family MUGILOIDIDAE

WEEVERS OR GRUBFISHES

Grubfishes are relatively small fishes with elongate, somewhat cylindrical bodies. They are bottom-dwellers that inhabit coral and rocky reefs, usually where there is some sand present. Many species occur in very shallow water (*i.e.*, less than 10 meters), but others are found down to depths of at least 50 meters. They are carnivorous feeders that remain stationary on the bottom for long periods, only occasionally swimming to a new position a short distance from the previous one. They are usually solitary in habit but sometimes occur in pairs or small groups.

Ten species have been collected in Western Australia; southern cool water species include *Parapercis allporti*, *P. haackei*, *P. naevosa*, and *P. ramsayi*. The wavy grubfish (*P. haackei*) is the most common inhabitant of shallow southern reefs. It ranges as far north as the Houtman Abrolhos. The spot head grubfish (*P. cephalopunctata*) and Ogilby's grubfish (*P. clathrata*) are common on reefs in the North West Cape area.

Families TRICHONOTIDAE, CREEDIDAE, and LEPTOSCOPIDAE

SANDFISHES

The three families in this group are represented by only five species in Western Australia. These fishes are adapted for burrowing. The snout of trichonotids and creedids is firm and pointed, thus facilitating head-first entries into the sand at the approach of danger. The sand lance (*Trichonotus setiger*) is an extremely elongate fish that grows to about 18 cm in length. It inhabits featureless sand beds in depths ranging from one to at least 10 meters. They appear to feed on plankton a short distance above the bottom. At the approach of a diver individual fish quickly dart into the sand. They usually bury themselves just below the surface, frequently leaving the snout and eyes exposed. Similar tactics are employed by the tommyfish (*Limnichthys fasciatus*), but because of its small size, cryptic coloration, and preference for staying on the bottom, it is rarely seen. Most individuals are under 5 cm. The species is basically tropical but ranges as far south as Perth, whereas the sand lance is known in Western Australia only from the Dampier Archipelago.

The sandfish (*Crapatalus arenarius*) is the only representative of the family Leptoscopidae in Western Australia. It is seldom seen, however, because of its habit of burrowing, its cryptic coloration, and its small size (to about 9 cm).

Family BLENNIIDAE

BLENNIES

The blennies are small, elongate fishes that inhabit inshore areas. They are primarily confined to tropical and subtropical seas, with the greatest abundance of species in the vast Indo-Pacific region. They are extremely abundant on shallow tidal flats composed of consolidated limestone and also in rocky surge pools. Most of the species are bottom-living forms that feed chiefly on algae.

The family ranks tenth in size for Western Australia with 37 species recorded. All except the Tasmanian blenny (*Parablennius* species), which is distributed south of Geraldton, are tropical forms. Most species are confined to shallow water, but members of the genera *Ecsenius*, *Aspidontus*, and *Plagiotremus* are also found to at least 15-20 meters depth. The species belonging to the two latter groups are especially interesting. Unlike most blennies, they are free-swimming forms that spend much of the time above the bottom. They are equipped with relatively large fang-like canine teeth adapted for tearing off small chunks of fins and scales from passing fishes. The false cleanerfish (*Aspidontus taeniatus*) is a nearly perfect mimic of the inoffensive cleaner wrasse (*Labroides dimidiatus*), both in color and behavior. It uses this disguise to approach within striking range of unsuspecting victims.

The four Western Australian species of *Ecsenius* are primarily dwellers of living coral reefs, although the lined blenny (*E. lineatus*) is sometimes found on consolidated limestone or rubble. The most common member of the genus is the bicolor blenny (*E. bicolor*), which exhibits two distinct color varieties, one that is half brown and half orange and another that is uniformly dark. Species belonging to *Entomacrodus*, *Istiblennius*, and *Salarias* are mostly confined to shallow reef flats and pools of the intertidal zone. *Omobranchus* and *Petroscirtes* are also shallow water inhabitants but generally prefer areas where there is considerable weed growth, although the former genus is also abundant in limestone rubble immediately adjacent to the shore. One of the most common species in northern waters is the dusky blenny (*Cirripectes filamentosus*), which occurs just below the surge zone to a depth of about 10-15 meters. The newest addition to the Western Australian blenniid fauna is *Stanulus talboti*, which was previously known only from the southern Great Barrier Reef. Several specimens were recently collected at North West Cape.

Families CONGROGADIDAE and NOTOGRAPTIDAE

EEL BLENNIES

The congrogadids and notograptids are eel-like fishes with extremely elongate, laterally compressed bodies. The dorsal and anal fins are very long, have numerous rays, and are confluent with the caudal fin. In addition, the scales are small and the pelvic fins are either absent or rudimentary. These fishes inhabit relatively shallow reef areas north of Carnarvon. All except the 60 cm *Congrogadus subducens* are small species under about 15 cm total length. Because of their cryptic habits they are seldom seen unless collected with rotenone ichthyocides. Six species, three from each family, are known from Western Australia.

Family TRIPTERYGIIDAE

TRIPLEFINS

The triplefins are blenny-like fishes that inhabit shallow seas of tropical and temperate latitudes. Both common and scientific family names allude to the presence of three distinct dorsal fins. Most of the members are tiny, not exceeding 7 cm in length. There are many species, but the group is poorly known and desperately needs revision.

Seventeen representatives have been collected in Western Australia; all except five are tropical forms that are mostly unidentified. The two temperate species are well known fishes that are especially abundant in shallow rocky areas. The jumping blenny (*Lepidoblennius marmoratus*) is one of the largest members of the family, growing to a length of about 12 cm. Like many of the tripterygiids, the black-throated threefin (*Helcogramma decurrens*) exhibits sexual color differences. The female is primarily mottled green, and mature males are jet black on the ventral half of the head and body. The threefin ranges southward of the Houtman Abrolhos.

Family CLINIDAE

SCALED BLENNIES OR WEEDFISHES AND SNAKE BLENNIES

The weedfishes obtain their common name from the habit of dwelling among seaweed. They are small, laterally compressed fishes that live along rocky coasts. There are about 75 species in the family, and most are confined to the Southern Hemisphere: approximately 40 occur in Australia. Most of the Australian representatives belong to the genus *Heteroclinus*. This is one of the three marine families in Western Australia that are livebearers, the others being Bythitidae and Ophidiidae. The true weedfishes include the genera *Cristiceps* and *Heteroclinus*; *Cristiceps* is distinguished from *Heteroclinus* by the more anterior placement of the first dorsal fin. In the former genus it is situated right above the eye, but in *Heteroclinus* it is well behind, usually above the gill cover. There are 15 species represented in these two genera, several of which are undescribed; most belong to *Heteroclinus*. The maximum length usually does not exceed 10 cm, but *Cristiceps* grows to about 22 cm.

Within a given species there is tremendous variation in color pattern, with reds, greens, and browns as the dominant theme.

The snake blennies were previously placed in a separate family (Ophiclinidae), but recent investigations reveal that they are modified weed fishes. There are 10 species represented in Western Australia belonging to four genera: *Ophiclinops, Ophiclinus, Peronedys,* and *Sticharium.* The preferred habitat is rocky reef areas and surge pools, usually where there is dense seaweed. The maximum size of these fishes is about 7-12 cm.

Family CALLIONYMIDAE

DRAGONETS

The dragonets are unusual looking fishes with an elongate body and flattened head. The cheek on most species is equipped with a prominent spine. They are benthic dwellers that range from shallow coastal pools to deep offshore waters. Most species prefer sandy habitats and exhibit colors that blend in well with their surroundings. They sometimes burrow into the sand, leaving only the slightly elevated eyes exposed. In some species the male has the rays of the first dorsal fin produced into greatly elongate filaments.

Eighteen species have been recorded from Western Australia, mainly from the tropical north. The most decorative of these by far is the ornate dragonet (*Synchiropus picturatus*). The species was described by Peters in 1876 and was reported as having come from Salawati Island, off western Irian Jaya. However, the type specimen was recently reexamined by R. McKay of the Queensland Museum, and he reports that the specimen label reads "Dirk Hartog Insel" (a large island forming the outer boundary of Shark Bay, Western Australia) as the collecting locality. Evidently the New Guinea location

is in error. The only other Western Australian specimens are three individuals collected by McKay at Rosemary Island in the Dampier Archipelago.

Perhaps the most common member of the family in Western Australia is the fingered dragonet (*Dactylopus dactylopus*), which inhabits sandy areas from Perth northward. This species, which grows to a length of about 20 cm, is larger than most callionymids.

Family GOBIIDAE

GOBIES

The gobies are perhaps the most abundant family in shallow tropical seas in terms of number of species. They exhibit a wide variety of shapes and sizes, although most are elongate, laterally compressed fishes under about 8 cm in length. There are two separate dorsal fins and the pelvic fins of many species are modified to form a disc apparatus. The group includes some of the smallest fishes in the world. For example, members of the genus *Pandaka* reach sexual maturity at between 10 to 15 mm total length. Most species prefer sandy habitats, either adjacent to coral reefs or in shallow coastal areas. Some are found mainly in estuaries and the lower reaches of freshwater streams. Although the gobies are primarily tropical, they are also represented in temperate seas.

The Gobiidae is the most speciose family in Western Australia; 90 species have been recorded to date and certainly more will be discovered in the future. Among the most interesting species are the shrimp gobies (genus *Cryptocentrus*), which share their sandy burrows with an alpheid shrimp. The shrimp continually excavates the dwelling place, keeping it free of large pebbles and debris. In turn, the fish provides protection for the shrimp by keeping a constant watch at the entrance to the burrow. It warns of approaching danger by making a rapid retreat into the sandy lair.

The Western Australian goby genera exemplify the wide range of habitats in which these fishes are found. *Gobiodon* and *Paragobiodon* dwell among the branches of live coral; *Eviota* shows a preference for corals, sponges, and gorgonians; *Valenciennea*, *Amblygobius*, *Cryptocentrus*, *Oplopomus*, and others live in sandy burrows; *Asterropteryx* dwells on dead coral surfaces; *Trimma* is found in caves; and *Glossogobius* exhibits an affinity for brackish water and also occurs in freshwater streams.

While most gobies are relatively sedentary bottom-dwellers, there are a few that are largely free-swimming, retreating to burrows or crevices only if danger threatens. These include *Ptereleotris evides* and *Parioglossus taeniatus*. The former species occurs in pairs or small aggregations that feed in midwater on zooplankton. *Parioglossus* forms large schools that swim in a peculiar vertically oriented fashion.

The common goby (*Bathygobius fuscus*) is perhaps the most abundant member of the family in northern waters. It occurs in surge pools and also in reef areas down to 10 meters. Like most gobies it is omnivorous, but it ingests primarily animal matter that includes crabs, shrimp, polychaetes, and juvenile fishes.

In southern waters, particularly around the Perth area, the long finned goby (*Favonigobius lateralis*) is very abundant over open sand next to shore. Literally hundreds can be seen in wading depths off Rockingham Beach at the southern end of Cockburn Sound.

The members of the subfamily Periophthalminae are unusual gobies commonly known as mudskippers. They dwell in shallow coastal areas, being particularly abundant where mangroves are found. They differ from other gobies by having the eyes elevated above the dorsal profile of the head and by the possession of limb-like pectoral fins. These are adaptations that enable the mudskippers to lead a semiterrestrial existence. They spend most of their time out of the water foraging for food or just resting on exposed mud flats or river banks. They move with a peculiar walking or sliding movement aided by their muscular pectoral fins. If disturbed they skip rapidly toward the water. Breathing while out of water is accomplished partly by absorption of oxygen through the peripheral blood vessels of the skin, but they are also able to store water in the gill cavity. The subfamily contains some of the largest known gobies, reaching lengths of up to 30 cm.

Family GOBIOIDIDAE

BLIND GOBIES

This is a small family with only two representatives in Western Australia, both from the extreme north. The worm goby (*Brachyamblyopus coecus*) looks just like its namesake. It is a 7 cm fish that is elongate, has few scales, has rudimentary fins, and is reddish pink in color. The eyes are also rudimentary, but they are really not needed in the murky environment inhabited by these fishes. They live in the thick, soupy mud of estuaries and the lower reaches of tidal rivers.

Family ACANTHURIDAE

SURGEONFISHES

The herbivorous surgeonfishes or tangs are primarily inhabitants of tropical coral reefs, although a few species range into temperate latitudes. There are approximately 60 to 70 species residing in both the Atlantic and Indo-Pacific regions. They are medium-sized fishes that are strongly compressed laterally. The most distinctive feature is the presence of one or more scalpel-like spines on each side of the tail base. In the genus *Acanthurus,* which is the largest in the family, the spines fold forward into a groove and can therefore be concealed when not used as a defensive weapon. Most other surgeonfish genera possess a similar apparatus, but the long-snout surgeons (genus *Naso*) have fixed spines or immobile bony tubercles. The caudal spines of all surgeonfishes are capable of inflicting deep, painful wounds unless handled with caution. A few species, such as the striped tang (*Acanthurus lineatus*), have a venom associated with the spines and wounds are extremely painful. Fifteen species have been recorded from Western Australia; of these the northwest surgeonfish (*Acanthurus grammoptilus*) is the most common. The distribution of this species is restricted to northwestern Australia. The yellow-eye surgeonfish (*Ctenochaetus strigosus*) is characterized by a bright yellow juvenile stage (sometimes called the Indo-Pacific yellow tang) that gradually changes to a somber shade of brown with increased growth. However, it does retain some yellow around the eye.

Family SIGANIDAE

RABBITFISHES

The rabbitfishes bear a strong resemblance to the surgeonfishes but differ by lacking the spines on the sides of the tail base. However, they are able to inflict venomous wounds with their fin spines and therefore, like the surgeonfishes, must be handled with extreme care. They are transient inhabitants of tropical reefs that usually travel in pairs or small to large schools. Some species prefer live coral reefs, but others are found where weed is the predominate bottom cover. Generally the weed-dwellers tend to form large schools and exhibit cryptic colors that blend in well with the surroundings; the whitespotted rabbitfish (*Siganus canaliculatus*) is a species that falls into this category.

There are eight species known from northern Western Australia. One of these, the three spot rabbitfish (*Siganus trispilos*), is a particularly attractive species that dwells on rich coral reefs of the Dampier Archipelago and North West Cape. Nearly as striking is the two barred rabbitfish (*Siganus doliatus*), which has a pattern of fine blue lines and a patch of brilliant yellow on the back. It is usually encountered in pairs on live coral reefs to depths of at least 15 meters.

Order PLEURONECTIFORMES

FLATFISHES

There is a bewildering variety of flatfish species in Western Australia, and the group is in bad need of taxonomic revision. Five families are represented that are easily separated on the basis of such features as body shape and the side of the body where both eyes are located. The young larvae of flatfishes are typical of most fish groups with regard to shape and behavior. In this stage there is one eye on each side of the head and the larvae swim in a normal position. However, this state of affairs does not last long as one eye gradually migrates to the other side of the head and the characteristic flatfish shape is assumed, with a blind unpigmented side that is always in contact with the sandy bottom. The tongue soles (family Cynoglossidae) are elongate flatfishes with the eyes on the left side and a distinctive rostral hook; the left-handed flounders (family Bothidae) have the eyes situated on the left side but are more ovate than the tongue soles; the right-handed flounders

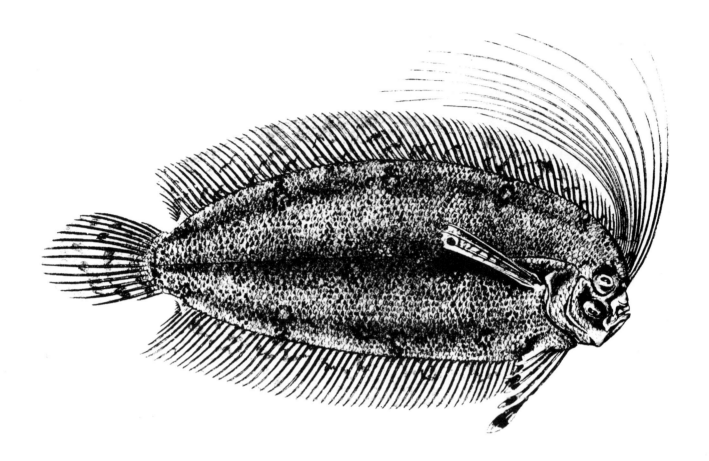

Samaris cacatuae Ogilby (family Pleuronectidae). From McCulloch & Whitley, 1925. *Rec. Aust. Mus.*, 14(4): Pl. 49.

(family Pleuronectidae) and soles (family Soleidae) have their eyes situated on the right side but are distinguished from each other by the lack of a free preopercular margin and a poorly developed lower jaw in the latter family. The toothed flounder (family Psettodidae) represents an anomaly in that the eyes are on the left side in some individuals and on the right in others; however, it is easily distinguished by the prominent jaw teeth and the position of the dorsal fin that originates well behind the eyes instead of in front of the eyes or directly over them as in most flatfishes.

Families MONACANTHIDAE and BALISTIDAE

LEATHERJACKETS AND TRIGGERFISHES

These distinctive families are closely related and are sometimes included together in the Balistidae. However, there appear to be significant differences to warrant their separation. Triggerfishes (Balistidae) tend to have larger scales that are arranged in regular rows and the fins contain branched rays as opposed to the simple rays of the leatherjackets (Monacanthidae). In addition, triggerfishes are usually heavier bodied; that is, they are not as laterally compressed as the leatherjackets. Both groups possess an ovate shape and have small mouths equipped with powerful jaws and relatively few teeth. Important characters found in both triggerfishes and leatherjackets include the triggerlike first dorsal spine and modified pelvics that are fused into a single spine. Most of the species are omnivorous, feeding on a wide variety of items that include algae, corals, sponges, molluscs, echinoderms, crustaceans, and polychaetes.

Nine species of triggerfishes are known from Western Australia; without exception they are restricted to tropical northern waters. The most common varieties are the brown trigger (*Sufflamen fraenatus*) and the golden-finned trigger (*S. chrysopterus*), which are especially abundant in the vicinity of North West Cape. Not nearly as common (but perhaps more conspicuous) is the blue-lined trigger (*Pseudobalistes fuscus*). Adults reach an enormous size (about 50 cm) and are very aggressive. The young go through a series of dramatic color changes that greatly enhance their popularity as aquarium fish.

The leatherjackets are well represented in Australia with approximately 55 species; many of these occur in temperate latitudes. Of the 38 species (making it the ninth largest family in the state) found in Western Australia, about half are southern forms that inhabit rocky reefs and sea grass beds. They range in size from the diminutive pygmy leatherjackets (genus *Brachaluteres*), which mature at a length of under 6 cm, to the tropical genus *Alutera*, which may grow to 60 cm or more.

The toothbrush leatherjacket (*Penicipelta vittiger*) receives its common name from the patch of close-set bristles below the dorsal fin of males. This species, which grows to about 30 cm, generally occurs in small schools in weedy areas. This is also the habitat of the rough leatherjacket (*Scobinichthys granulatus*), which is characterized by numerous fleshy flaps covering the body.

The blue-lined leatherjacket (*Meuschenia galii*) is found on rocky reefs and possesses the ability to change color rapidly. It may suddenly switch from an overall greenish brown to a colorful pattern consisting of numerous light blue spots and stripes. The maximum size of the species is about 35 cm. The horseshoe leatherjacket (*Meuschenia hippocrepis*) and the mosaic leatherjacket (*Eubalichthys mosaicus*) are found in caves and under ledges on southern rocky reefs. These species are relatively large, reaching a maximum length between 40 and 50 cm. The latter species is particularly beautiful with bright yellow spots and stripes on a pale blue background.

Perhaps the most widespread monacanthid in Western Australia is the fan-bellied leatherjacket (*Monacanthus chinensis*), which ranges from Geographe Bay to the extreme northern portion of the state. It has a prominent flap of skin extending from the pelvic tip to the anal region.

The redtail leatherjacket (*Pervagor janthinosoma*) is a common monacanthid on northern coral reefs. It is a shy fish that seldom wanders far from protective shelter. The species is relatively small, attaining a maximum length of about 12 cm.

Family OSTRACIONTIDAE

BOXFISHES

The boxfishes are an unmistakable group characterized by an external carapace consisting of bony plates. They are generally poor swimmers that rely mainly on their armor for protection from potential predators. Some species produce a toxic mucus that can kill other fishes kept in the same container. Many aquarists have learned this fact the hard way. Most individuals collected or observed are under 20 cm in length; however, several species including the popular polka dot boxfish (*Ostracion cubicus*) grow to over 40 cm. Dietary items include algae, polychaetes, molluscs, crustaceans, and small fishes. Seventeen species have been collected in Western Australia, the majority from southern latitudes. A few of these are extremely ornate. Shaw's cowfish (*Aracana aurita*) occurs on rocky reefs and exhibits a maze of wavy brown lines on a background of red and white. Equally attractive is the white-barred boxfish (*Anoplocapros lenticularis*), which is bright red-orange with white bars. It is chiefly a cavern dweller and is not uncommon in the Perth area.

Families TETRAODONTIDAE and DIODONTIDAE

PUFFERFISHES AND PORCUPINEFISHES

The puffers and porcupinefishes are well known for the ability to inflate their body several times the normal size when taken from the water or when exposed to other stressful conditions. The skin is highly elastic and swelling is achieved by swallowing water or air. Porcupinefishes differ from puffers by the presence of conspicuous spines embedded in the skin. In addition, the teeth are fused into an undivided beak, whereas the fused teeth of puffers are split at the front of the jaws. The food of these fishes consists largely of gastropods, crustaceans, polychaetes, sponges, and algae.

The pufferfishes are represented by 25 species in Western Australia; most are inhabitants of northern reefs, preferring areas of sand or mud bottom. One of the most abundant species in the cool temperate waters south of the Abrolhos Islands is the common blowfish (*Torquigener pleurogramma*). It occurs in very large schools and is a continual nuisance to fishermen because of its habit of either becoming hooked or stealing the bait. The ringed puffer (*Omegophora armilla*) is a less common southern species. It is solitary in habit and sometimes buries itself partially in the sand.

The dominant tetraodontid of tropical reefs is the broad-barred puffer (*Arothron hispidus*), which ranges widely in the Indo-Pacific region. Another common species that prefers mud flats rather than coral reefs is the narrow-lined puffer (*A. immaculatus*). These species range in size from about 30-50 cm total length.

Six species of porcupinefishes are recorded from Western Australia. The globefish (*Diodon nicthemerus*) and small-spined porcupinefish (*Allomycterus pilatus*) inhabit southern waters and are easily separated. The former species has very long spines covering the body that are erected when the body is inflated, in contrast to the short immovable spines of *A. pilatus*. The northern porcupinefishes, which have immovable spines with three root-like branches at their base, belong to the genus *Chilomycterus* and are readily distinguished from *Diodon*, also a tropical genus, which has erectile spines that have two basal branches.

2. Rocky headlands meet the cold, clear waters of the Southern Ocean near the entrance to King George Sound, Western Australia.

3. "Sugarloaf," a prominent landmark near Cape Naturaliste, Western Australia.

4. Aerial view of Beacon Island and surrounding reefs, Wallabi Group, Houtman Abrolhos.

5. A northern coral reef at Rosemary Island, Dampier Archipelago.

6. Port Jackson shark, *Heterodontus portusjacksoni* Meyer, about 120 cm TL (total length), taken at a depth of about 10 meters.

7. Speckled catshark, *Hemiscyllium trispeculare* Richardson, about 60 cm TL, at Kendrew Island, Dampier Archipelago, in 2 meters depth.

8. Gulf wobbegong, *Orectolobus halei* Whitley, about 65 cm TL, at Geographe Bay in 10 meters depth.

9. Northern wobbegong, *Orectolobus wardi* Whitley, about 50 cm TL, at Kendrew Island, Dampier Archipelago, in about 3 meters depth.

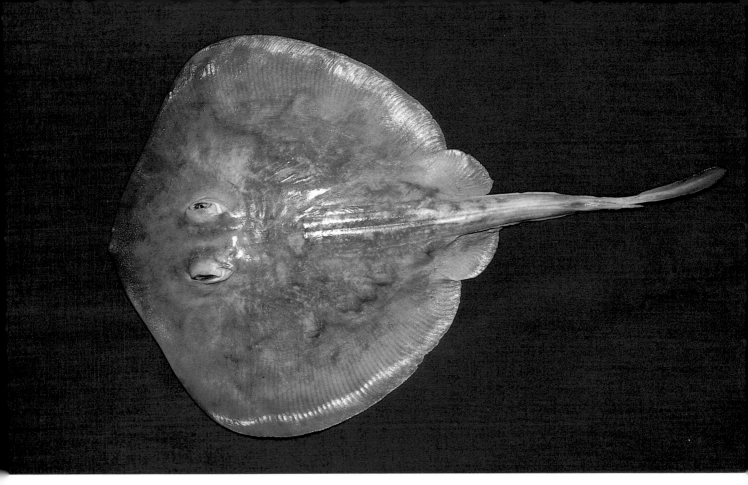

10. Lobed stingaree, *Urolophus lobatus* McKay, 205 cm disc width, taken off Port Peron from a depth of 30 meters.

11. Ambon shark, *Carcharhinus amboinensis* (Mueller & Henle), 150 cm TL, from Prince Regent River at a depth of 3 meters.

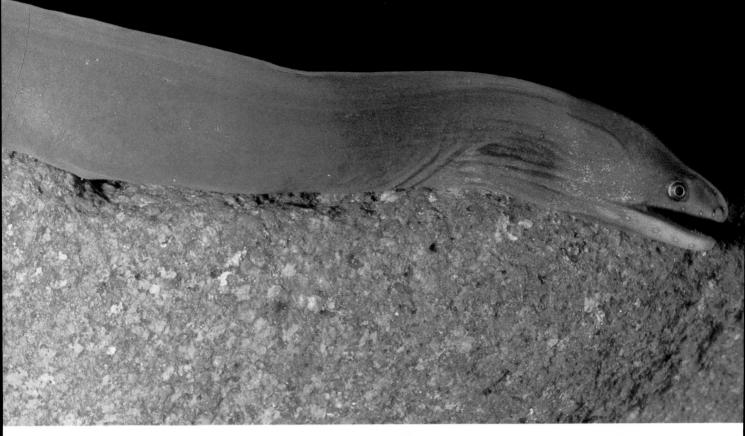

12. Brown moray, *Gymnothorax prasinus* (Richardson), 25 cm TL, from Geographe Bay at a depth of 3 meters.

13. Spotted moray, *Gymnothorax eurostus* (Abbott), about 50 cm TL, from Kendrew Island, Dampier Archipelago, in about 5 meters depth.

14. Freckled moray, *Gymnothorax thyrsoideus* (Richardson), about 28 cm TL, from Kendrew Island, Dampier Archipelago, in 2 meters depth.

15. Masked moray, *Gymnothorax* species, about 60 cm TL, from Rosemary Island, Dampier Archipelago, in 4 meters depth.

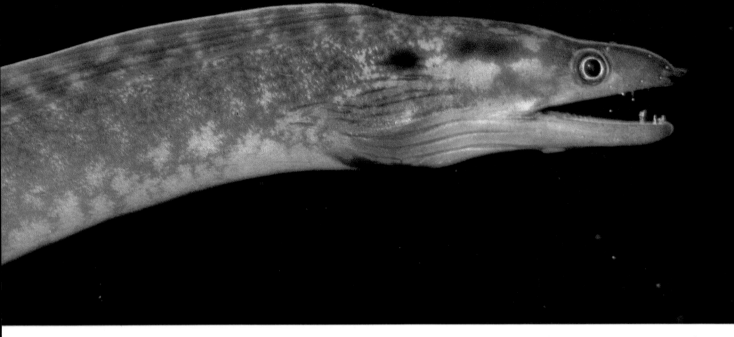

16. Tropical moray, *Gymnothorax margaritophora* (Bleeker), 50 cm TL, Christmas Island, Indian Ocean, from a depth of 6 meters.

17. Peppered moray, *Gymnothorax pictus* (Ahl), about 80 cm TL, from Christmas Island, Indian Ocean, at one meter depth.

18. Woodward's moray, *Gymnothorax woodwardi* McCulloch, about 75 cm TL, from Houtman Abrolhos, in 5 meters depth.

19. Starry eel, *Echidna nebulosa* (Ahl), about 90 cm TL, from Christmas Island, Indian Ocean, in 10 meters depth.

20. Southern conger eel, *Conger wilsoni* (Bloch & Schneider), 22 cm TL, from Geographe Bay, in 2 meters depth.

21. Ashen conger, *Conger cinereus* Rueppell, about 40 cm TL, from Kendrew Island, Dampier Archipelago, in a depth of 5 meters.

22. Tasmanian snake eel, *Muraenichthys tasmaniensis* McCulloch, 28 cm TL, from Geographe Bay, at a depth of 4 meters.

23. Southern burrowing snake eel, *Muraenichthys australis* Macleay, 20 cm TL, from Geographe Bay, at 6 meters depth.

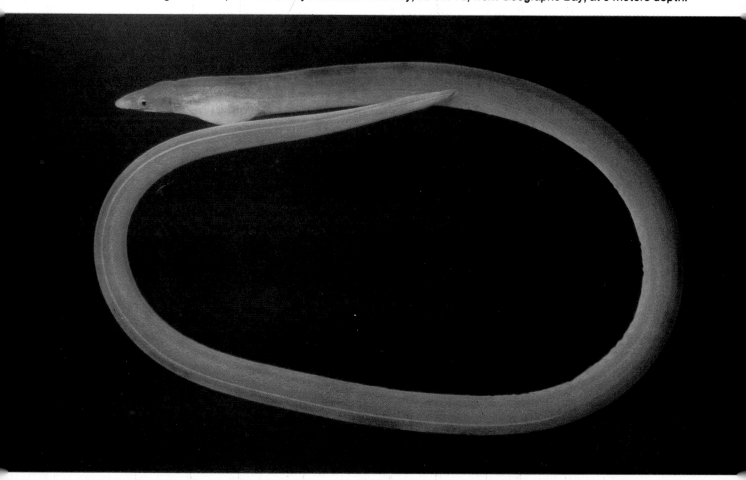

24. Burrowing snake eel, *Pisodonophis cancrivorus* (Richardson), 25 cm TL, from West Lewis Island, Dampier Archipelago, at 2 meters depth.

25. Ghost snake eel, *Brachysomophis cirrhocheilos* (Bleeker), about 110 cm TL, from Christmas Island, Indian Ocean, in 10 meters depth.

26. Scaly mackerel,
*Amblygaster
leiogaster*
(Valenciennes),
18 cm TL, from
Houtman
Abrolhos, from
10 meters
depth.

27. Blue sprat,
*Spratelloides
robustus*
Ogilby, 8 cm
TL, Houtman
Abrolhos, from
a depth of 5
meters.

28. Slender sprat,
*Spratelloides
gracilis*
(Schlegel), 7
cm TL, from
Houtman
Abrolhos, at a
depth of 5
meters.

29. Hamilton's an-
chovy, *Thryssa
hamiltoni*
(Gray), 7 cm TL,
from Prince
Regent River,
at a depth of
one meter.

30. Variegated lizardfish, *Synodus variegatus* (Lacepede), about 15 cm TL, from Kendrew Island, Dampier Archipelago, at a depth of 4 meters.

31. Slender lizardfish, *Saurida gracilis* Quoy & Gaimard, 16 cm TL, from North West Cape, taken from a depth of 25 meters.

32. Sergeant baker, *Aulopus purpurissatus* Richardson, about 12 cm TL, from Recherche Archipelago, at a depth of 12 meters.

33. Devil frogfish, *Halophryne diemensis* (Le Sueur), about 18 cm TL, from Lady Nora Island, Dampier Archipelago, at 3 meters depth.

34. White-lipped catfish, *Paraplotosus albilabrus* (Valenciennes), about 12 cm TL, Lady Nora Island, Dampier Archipelago, at a depth of 3 meters.

35. Black sailfin catfish, *Paraplotosus* sp. nov., 11 cm TL, from North West Cape, from 3 meters depth.

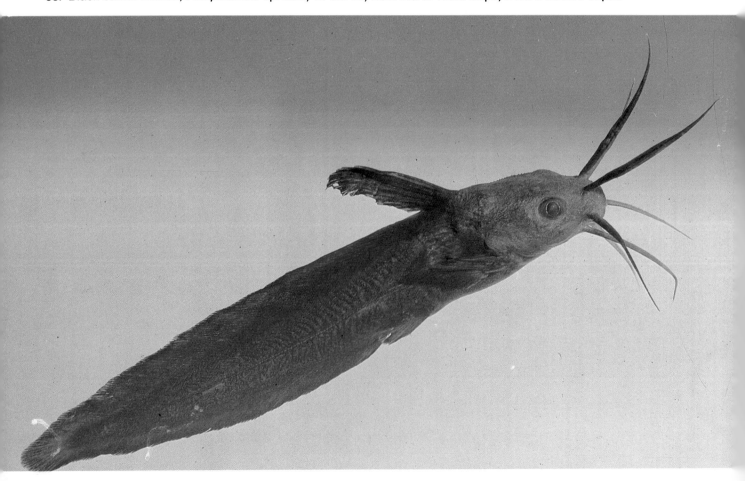

36. Forktail catfish, *Arius graeffei* Kner & Steindachner, 20 cm TL, from Prince Regent River, from a depth of 2 meters.

37. Cobbler, *Cnidoglanis macrocephalus* (Valenciennes), about 17 cm TL, from Point Peron, at a depth of 3 meters.

38. *Cochleoceps spatula*
(Guenther), 2.5 cm TL,
from Cockburn Sound,
Western Australia.

39. Tasmanian clingfish,
*Aspasmogaster tasma-
niensis* (Guenther), 7 cm
TL, from Geographe Bay,
from one meter depth.

40. Tasmanian clingfish,
*Aspasmogaster tasma-
niensis* (Guenther), 1.5 cm
TL, from Geographe Bay,
from one meter depth.

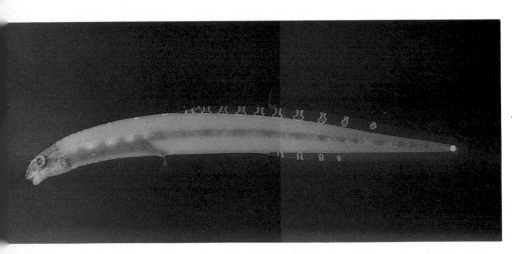

41. Eel clingfish, *Alabes parvulus* (McCulloch), 3.2 cm
TL, from Point Peron,
from a depth of 10
meters.

42. Yellow frogfish, *Antennarius nummifer* (Cuvier), 4 cm TL, from North West Cape, from a depth of 3 meters.

43. Spot tail frogfish, *Lophiocharon trisignatus* (Richardson), 14 cm TL, from Perth district, from a depth of 4 meters. Note the large egg mass attached to its side.

44. Tasseled frogfish, *Rhycherus gloveri* Pietsch, 15 cm TL, from Perth district, from a depth of 5 meters.

45. Butler's frogfish, *Tathicarpus butleri* Ogilby, 13 cm TL, from Carnarvon, from a depth of 10 meters.

46. Smooth frogfish, *Histiophryne bougainvilli* (Valenciennes), 3.5 cm TL, from a depth of 10 meters at Recherche Archipelago.

47. Beardie, *Lotella fuliginosa* (Guenther), 10 cm TL, from Garden Island at a depth of 5 meters.

48. Red cusk-eel, *Ogilbia* sp., about 9 cm TL, from Kendrew Island, Dampier Archipelago, in 10 meters depth.

49. Orange eelpout, *Dinematichthys dasyrhynchus* Cohen and Hutchins, about 8 cm TL, from Garden Island at a depth of 10 meters.

50. Bearded rock cod,
    *Pseudophycis
    breviusculus* Richardson,
    7 cm TL, from Geographe
    Bay at a depth of 4
    meters.

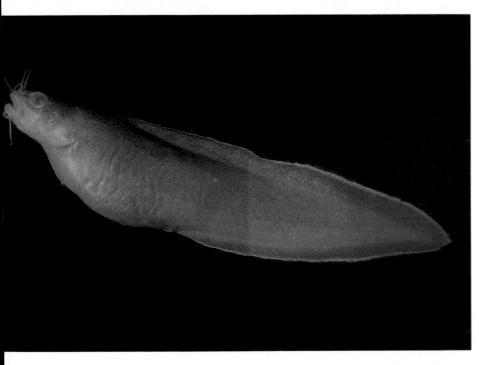

51. Barbeled cusk-eel, *Brotula
    multibarbata* Temminck &
    Schlegel, 12 cm TL, from
    Barrow Island, from a
    depth of 132 meters.

52. Cave cuck-eel, *Ogilbia*
    sp., 3.5 cm TL, from
    Garden Island, from a
    depth of 8 meters.

53. Southern sea garfish, *Hyporhamphus melanochir* (Valenciennes), 25 cm TL, from surface waters of Geographe Bay.

54. Black barred garfish, *Hemiramphus far* (Forsskal), 30 cm TL, from surface waters of Kendrew Island, Dampier Archipelago.

55. Dussumier's garfish, *Hyporhamphus dussumieri* (Valenciennes), 18 cm TL, from one meter depth at Houtman Abrolhos.

56. Elongate hardyhead, *Atherinosoma elongata* (Klunzinger), 7 cm TL, from one meter depth at Geographe Bay.

57. Few-rayed hardyhead, *Craterocephalus pauciradiatus* (Guenther), 6 cm TL, from one meter depth at North West Cape.

58. Surge silverside, *Iso rhothophilus* (Ogilby), 3 cm TL, from one meter depth at Geographe Bay.

59. Spotted hardyhead, *Pranesus endrachtensis* (Quoy & Gaimard), about 10 cm TL, from 2 meters depth at Rosemary Island, Dampier Archipelago.

60. Black-tip hardyhead, *Pranesus ogilbyi* Whitley, 8.5 cm TL, from 2 meters depth at Geographe Bay.

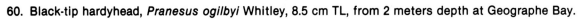

61. Swallowtail, *Centroberyx lineatus* (Cuvier), about 14 cm TL, from 20 meters depth at Geographe Bay. (Reddish fish in foreground.)

62. Knightfish, *Cleidopus gloriamaris* De Vis, 13 cm TL, from 2 meters depth at Houtman Abrolhos.

63. Roughy, *Trachichthys australis* Shaw & Nodder, about 12 cm TL, from 10 meters depth at Recherche Archipelago.

64. Little pineapple fish, *Sorosichthys ananassa* Whitley, 3 cm TL, from 10 meters depth at Recherche Archipelago.

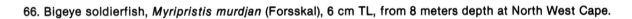

65. Hexagon soldierfish, *Myripristis hexagonatus* (Lacepede), about 15 cm TL, from 10 meters depth at Kendrew Island, Dampier Archipelago.

66. Bigeye soldierfish, *Myripristis murdjan* (Forsskal), 6 cm TL, from 8 meters depth at North West Cape.

67. Red-lined squirrelfish, *Sargocentron ruber* (Forsskal), about 18 cm TL, from 10 meters depth at Kendrew Island, Dampier Archipelago.

68. Violet squirrelfish, *Sargocentron violaceus* (Bleeker), about 30 cm TL, from 10 meters depth at Kendrew Island, Dampier Archipelago.

69. Janss' pipefish,
Doryrhamphus janssi
(Herald & Randall), about
10 cm TL, at 8 meters
depth at Kendrew Island,
Dampier Archipelago.

70. Mangrove pipefish,
*Parasyngnathus
argyrostictus* (Kaup), 12
cm TL, from one meter
depth at West Lewis
Island, Dampier Ar-
chipelago.

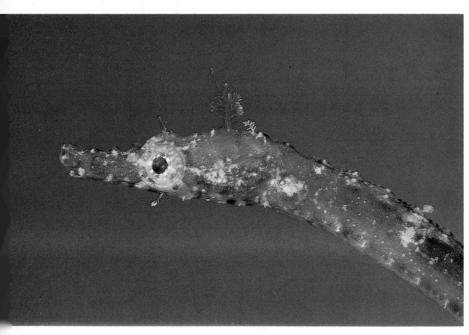

71. Gray's pipefish,
Halicampus grayi Kaup, 8
cm TL, from 15 meters
depth at Abrolhos
Islands, Western
Australia.

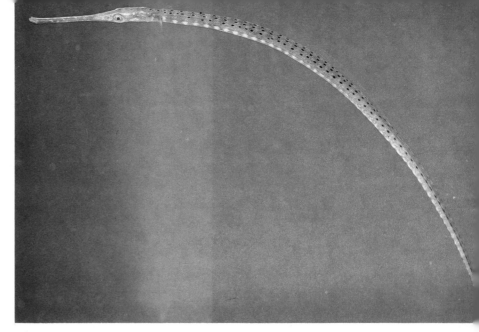

72. Peacock pipefish, *Stigmatopora argus* (Richardson), 12 cm TL, from 5 meters depth at Cockburn Sound.

73. Wide-bodied pipefish, *Stigmatopora nigra* Kaup, 7 cm TL, from 5 meters depth at Cockburn Sound.

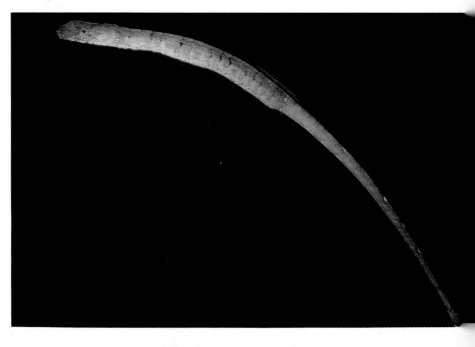

74. Crested pipefish, *Histiogamphelus cristatus* (Macleay), 12 cm TL, from 4 meters depth at Geographe Bay.

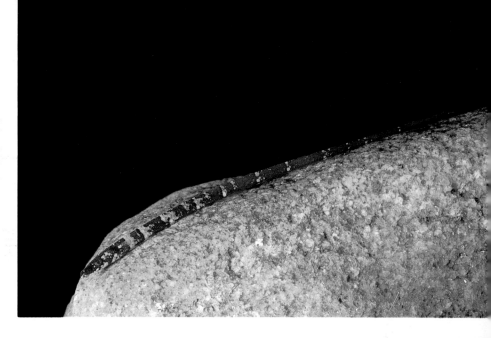

75. Smooth pipefish, *Lissocampus runa* (Whitley), 7 cm TL, from 4 meters depth at Geographe Bay.

76. Smooth pipefish, *Lissocampus runa* (Whitley), 7.8 cm TL, from 5 meters depth at Geographe Bay.

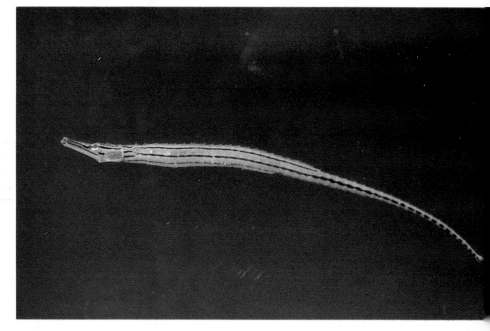

77. Maroubra pipefish, *Maroubra perserrata* Whitley, 6 cm TL, from 5 meters depth at Geographe Bay.

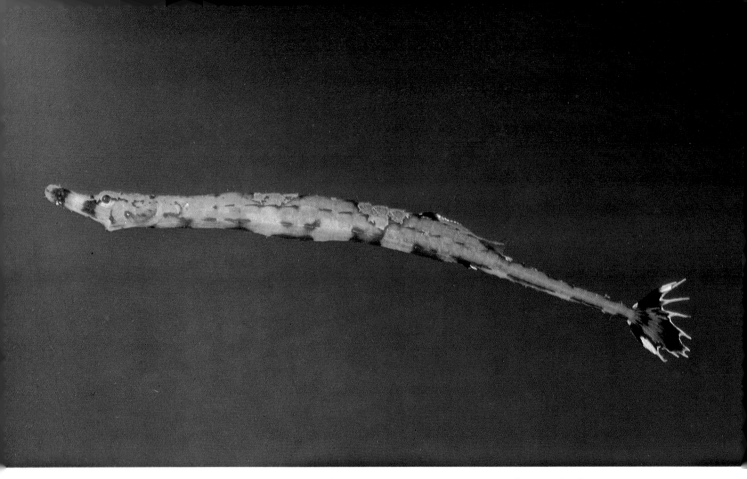

78. Herald's pipefish, *Heraldia nocturna* Paxton, 8 cm TL, from 5 meters depth at Geographe Bay.

79. Eel pipefish, *Bulbonaricus brauni* (Dawson & Allen), 5.5 cm TL, from 5 meters depth at North West Cape.

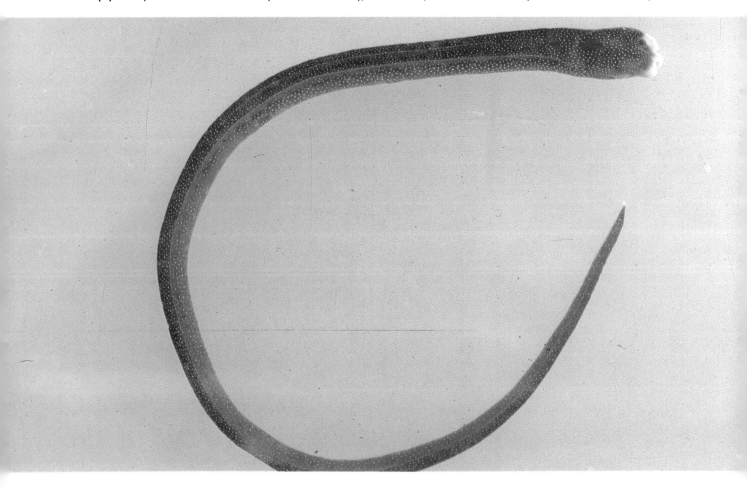

80. Spiny seahorse, *Hippocampus angustus* Guenther, 8 cm TL, from 10 meters depth at Cockburn Sound.

81. Knobby seahorse, *Hippocampus breviceps* Peters, 6.5 cm TL, from 20 meters depth off Point Peron.

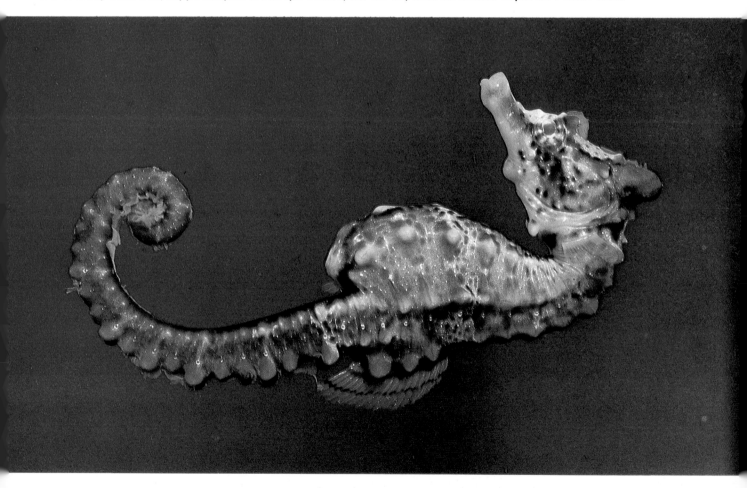

82. Leafy sea dragon, *Phycodurus eques* (Guenther), about 35 cm TL, in 15 meters depth at Recherche Archipelago.

83. Weedy sea dragon, *Phyllopteryx taeniolatus* (Lacepede), 37 cm TL, from Bass Point, New South Wales. Photo by Rudie Kuiter.

84. Weedy sea dragon, *Phyllopteryx taeniolatus* (Lacepede), 7 cm TL, from Sydney, New South Wales. Photo by Rudie Kuiter.

85. Ghost pipefish, *Solenichthys cyanopterus* (Bleeker), 8 cm TL, from Seal Rocks, New South Wales. Photo by Rudie Kuiter.

86. Zebra lionfish, *Dendrochirus zebra* (Quoy & Gaimard), about 18 cm TL, from 5 meters depth at Christmas Island, Indian Ocean.

87. Spotfin lionfish, *Pterois antennata* (Bloch), about 15 cm TL, from 8 meters depth at Christmas Island, Indian Ocean.

88. Northern scorpionfish, *Scorpaena picta* Cuvier, about 12 cm TL, from 10 meters depth at Kendrew Island, Dampier Archipelago.

89. Northern scorpionfish, *Scorpaena picta* Cuvier, about 10 cm TL, from 5 meters depth at Kendrew Island, Dampier Archipelago.

90. Ornate scorpionfish, *Scorpaenodes varipinnis* Smith, about 5 cm TL, from 10 meters depth at North West Cape.

91. Steene's scorpionfish, *Scorpaenodes steenei* Allen, about 18 cm TL, in 5 meters depth at Houtman Abrolhos.

92. Slender scorpionfish, *Scorpaenopsis cirrhosa* (Thunberg), 10 cm TL, from 10 meters depth at North West Cape.

93. False stonefish, *Scorpaenopsis diabolus* (Cuvier), about 8 cm TL, in 2 meters depth at Kendrew Island, Dampier Archipelago.

94. Little scorpion cod, *Scorpaenodes* sp., 10 cm TL, from 8 meters depth at North West Cape.

95. Little scorpion cod, *Scorpaenodes* sp., 8 cm TL, from 3 meters depth at North West Cape.

96. Devilfish, *Gymnapistes marmoratus* (Cuvier), 8 cm TL, from 3 meters depth at Cockburn Sound.

97. Gurnard scorpion perch, *Neosebastes pandus* (Richardson), 30 cm TL, from one meter depth at Mandurah.

98. Red scorpionfish, *Scorpaena sumptuosa* Castelnau, 30 cm TL, from 10 meters depth at Carnac Island.

99. Dampier stonefish, *Dampierosa daruma* Whitley, 10 cm TL, from 15 meters depth at Broome.

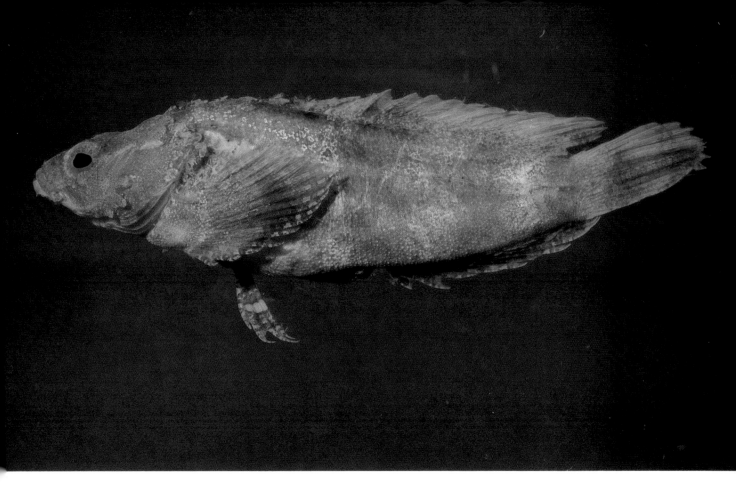

100. Cod scorpionfish, *Peristrominous dolosus* Whitley, 8 cm TL, from 12 meters depth at Onslow.

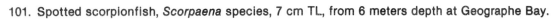

101. Spotted scorpionfish, *Scorpaena* species, 7 cm TL, from 6 meters depth at Geographe Bay.

102. Striped scorpionfish, *Minous monodactylus* (Bloch & Schneider), 8 cm TL, from 15 meters depth at Shark Bay.

103. Waspfish, *Paracentropogon vespa* Ogilby, 7 cm TL, from 15 meters depth at Shark Bay.

104. One-spot waspfish, *Liocranium praepositum* Ogilby, 10 cm TL, from a depth of 80 meters at Rowley Shoals.

105. Cockatoo waspfish, *Ablabys taenianotus* (Cuvier), 9 cm TL, from 3 meters depth at North West Cape.

106. Red Indianfish, *Pataecus fronto* Richardson, 12 cm TL, from 20 meters depth at Shark Bay.

107. Whiskered prowfish, *Neopataecus waterhousii* (Castelnau), 6 cm TL, from 10 meters depth at Cockburn Sound.

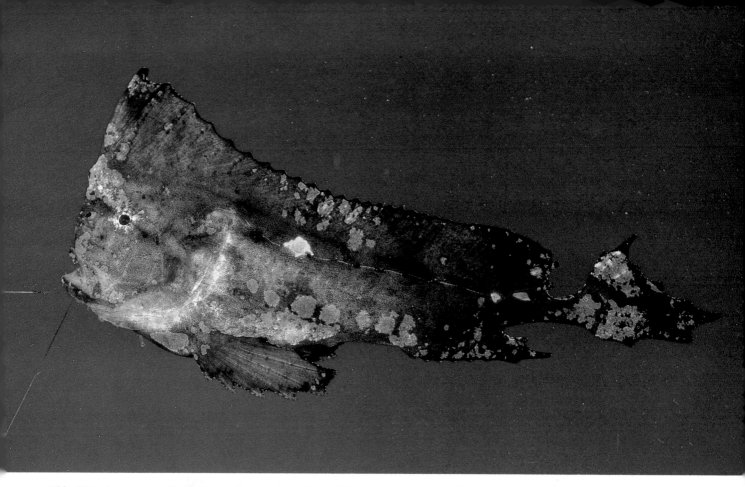

108. Whiskered prowfish, *Neopataecus waterhousii* (Castelnau), 4.8 cm TL, from 20 meters depth off Point Peron.

109. Pigfish, *Congiopodus leucometopon* (Waite), about 17 cm TL, from 10 meters depth at Recherche Archipelago.

110. Goblin scorpionfish, *Inimicus sinensis* (Valenciennes), about 35 cm TL, from 20 meters depth at Houtman Abrolhos.

111. Goblinfish, *Glyptauchen panduratus* (Richardson), about 10 cm TL, from 10 meters depth at Recherche Archipelago.

112. Seamoth, *Parapegasus natans* (Linnaeus), 10 cm TL, from 10 meters depth at Cockburn Sound.

113. Glass perch, *Ambassis interrupta* Bleeker, 5 cm TL, from one meter depth, Prince Regent River.

114. Barramundi, *Lates calcarifer* (Bloch), 50 cm TL, from one meter depth, Cape York Peninsula, Queensland.

115. Sand Bass, *Psammoperca waigiensis* (Cuvier), 28 cm TL, from 4 meters depth, North West Cape.

116. Giant grouper, *Promicrops lanceolatus* (Bloch), 30 cm TL, from 5 meters depth, Dampier Archipelago.

117. Barramundi cod, *Cromileptes altivelis* (Valenciennes), about 15 cm TL, from 3 meters depth, Rosemary Island, Dampier Archipelago.

118. Pink grouper, *Cephalopholis* sp., 9 cm TL, from 132 meters depth, Barrow Island.

119. Chinaman grouper, *Epinephelus rivulatus* (Valenciennes), about 25 cm TL, from 10 meters depth, North West Cape.

120. Coral grouper, *Epinephelus corallicola* (Valenciennes), about 23 cm TL, from 5 meters depth, Lady Nora Island, Dampier Archipelago.

121. Spotted grouper, possibly *Epinephelus maculatus* (Bloch), about 23 cm TL, from 4 meters depth, Rosemary Island, Dampier Archipelago.

122. Northwest grouper, *Epinephelus multinotatus* (Peters), about 40 cm TL, from 12 meters depth, North West Cape.

123. Rainford's perch, *Rainfordia opercularis* McCulloch, about 12 cm TL, from 10 meters depth, Kendrew Island, Dampier Archipelago.

124. Little fairy basslet, *Sacura parva* Heemstra & Randall, 7 cm TL, from 132 meters depth, Barrow Island.

125. Deepsea fairy basslet, *Anthias rubrizonatus* Randall, 12 cm TL, from 132 meters depth, Barrow Island.

126. Red fairy basslet, *Anthias kashiwae* (Tanaka), 9 cm TL, from 15 meters depth, North West Cape.

127. Red fairy basslet, *Anthias kashiwae* (Tanaka), 10 cm TL, from 12 meters depth, North West Cape.

128. Barber perch, *Caesioperca rasor* (Richardson), male about 24 cm TL, in 20 meters depth, Recherche Archipelago.

129. Barber perch, *Caesioperca rasor* (Richardson), female about 18 cm TL, in 20 meters depth, Recherche Archipelago.

130. Harlequinfish, *Othos dentex* (Cuvier), about 70 cm TL, in 18 meters depth, Recherche Archipelago.

131. Breaksea cod, *Epinephelides armatus* (Castelnau), about 28 cm TL, in 10 meters depth, Geographe Bay.

132. Red seaperch, *Ellerkeldia rubra* Allen, 9 cm TL, from 3 meters depth, Houtman Abrolhos.

133. Western seaperch, *Ellerkeldia wilsoni* Allen and Moyer, about 20 cm TL, in 15 meters depth, Geographe Bay.

134. Wirrah, *Acanthistius serratus* (Cuvier), 8 cm TL, from one meter depth, Geographe Bay.

135. Black banded seaperch, *Hypoplectrodes nigrorubrum* (Cuvier), about 9 cm TL, in 8 meters depth, Esperance.

136. Banded longfin, *Belonepterygium fasciolatum* (Ogilby), 5 cm TL, from 3 meters depth, North West Cape.

137. False gramma, *Pseudogramma polyacantha* (Bleeker), about 5 cm TL, in 2 meters depth, Kendrew Island, Dampier Archipelago.

138. Rose devilfish, *Pseudoplesiops rosae* Schultz, 5 cm TL, from 10 meters depth, North West Cape.

139. Northern devilfish, *Plesiops coeruleolineatus* Rueppell, 3.5 cm TL, from 3 meters depth, North West Cape.

140. Western blue devil, *Paraplesiops meleagris* Peters, about 25 cm TL, in 12 meters depth, Recherche Archipelago.

141. Western blue devil, *Paraplesiops meleagris* Peters, about 20 cm TL, in 12 meters depth, Recherche Archipelago.

142. Braun's hula-fish, *Trachinops brauni* Allen, about 5 cm TL, in 10 meters depth, Recherche Archipelago.

143. Braun's hula-fish, *Trachinops brauni* Allen, about 6 cm TL, Rottnest Island.

144. Southern hula-fish, *Trachinops noarlungae* Glover, about 9 cm TL, in 10 meters depth, Rottnest Island.

145. Lined cichlops, *Labracinus lineatus* (Castelnau), 14 cm TL, from 5 meters depth, Houtman Abrolhos.

146. Lined cichlops, *Labracinus lineatus* (Castelnau), about 20 cm TL, in 10 meters depth, Houtman Abrolhos.

147. Dusky dottyback (yellow variety), *Pseudochromis fuscus* Mueller & Troschel, 7 cm TL, from 3 meters depth, Rosemary Island, Dampier Archipelago.

148. Dusky dottyback (dark variety), *Pseudochromis fuscus* Mueller & Troschel, about 7 cm TL, in 3 meters depth, Rosemary Island, Dampier Archipelago.

149. Yellowhead dottyback, *Pseudochromis tapeinosoma* Bleeker, male 5 cm TL, from 10 meters depth, North West Cape.

150. Yellowhead dottyback, *Pseudochromis tapeinosoma* Bleeker, female 4 cm TL, from 10 meters depth, North West Cape.

151. Yellowfin dottyback, *Pseudochromis wilsoni* Whitley, male about 6 cm TL, in 20 meters depth, Houtman Abrolhos.

152. **Yellowfin dottyback,** *Pseudochromis wilsoni* **Whitley, a female 6 cm TL, from 6 meters depth, Rosemary Island, Dampier Archipelago.**

153. **Marshalls dottyback,** *Pseudochromis marshallensis* **Schultz, 7 cm TL, from 10 meters depth, North West Cape.**

154. West Australian jewfish, *Glaucosoma hebraicum* Richardson, about 60 cm TL, in 12 meters depth, Houtman Abrolhos.

155. Striped perch, *Helotes sexlineatus* Quoy & Gaimard, 12 cm TL, from 2 meters depth, Cockburn Sound.

156. Four-lined perch, *Pelates quadrilineatus* (Bloch), 5 cm TL, from 2 meters depth, Rosemary Island, Dampier Archipelago.

157. Yellowtail, *Amniataba caudavittatus* (Richardson), 9 cm TL, from one meter depth, Maitland River.

158. Little red cardinalfish, *Apogon coccineus* Rueppell, about 6 cm TL, in 3 meters depth, Kendrew Island, Dampier Archipelago.

159. Cook's cardinalfish, *Apogon cooki* Macleay, about 7 cm TL, in 8 meters depth, Kendrew Island, Dampier Archipelago.

160. Doederlein's cardinalfish, *Apogon doederleini* Jordan & Snyder, about 7 cm TL, in 15 meters depth, Houtman, Abrolhos.

161. Pink-striped cardinalfish, *Apogon* species, about 10 cm TL, in 6 meters depth, North West Cape.

162. Darnley cardinalfish, *Apogon darnleyensis* Alleyne & Macleay, about 5 cm TL, from 10 meters depth, North West Cape.

163. Hartzfeld's cardinalfish, *Apogon hartzfeldi* Bleeker, about 7 cm TL, in 4 meters depth, Rosemary Island, Dampier Archipelago.

164. Big red cardinalfish, *Apogon crassiceps* Garman, about 10 cm TL, in 10 meters depth, Kendrew Island, Dampier Archipelago.

165. Gobbleguts, *Apogon ruppelli* Guenther, about 10 cm TL, in 8 meters depth, Geographe Bay.

166. Oblique banded cardinalfish, *Apogon semiornatus* Peters, 8 cm TL, from 12 meters depth, North West Cape.

167. Black spot cardinalfish, *Archamia melasma* Lachner & Taylor, 7 cm TL, from 5 meters depth, Rosemary Island, Dampier Archipelago.

168. Lachner's cardinalfish, *Cheilodipterus lachneri* Klausewitz, about 11 cm TL, in 4 meters depth, North West Cape.

169. Candystriped cardinalfish, *Cheilodipterus lineatus* Lacepede, about 14 cm TL, in 10 meters depth, Kendrew Island, Dampier Archipelago.

170. Samoan cardinalfish, *Foa fo* Jordan & Seale, 3 cm TL, from 7 meters depth, North West Cape.

171. Barred cardinalfish, *Fowleria variegata* (Valenciennes), 4 cm TL, from 5 meters depth, North West Cape.

172. Slender cardinalfish, *Rhabdamia* species, 4 cm TL, from 15 meters depth, Houtman Abrolhos.

173. Blacknosed cardinalfish, *Rhabdamia cypselurus* Weber, 5 cm TL, from 12 meters depth, North West Cape.

174. Silver belly, *Rhabdamia gracilis* (Bleeker), 5 cm TL, from 15 meters depth, North West Cape.

175. Silver belly, *Rhabdamia gracilis* (Bleeker), about 5-6 cm TL, in 12 meters depth, North West Cape.

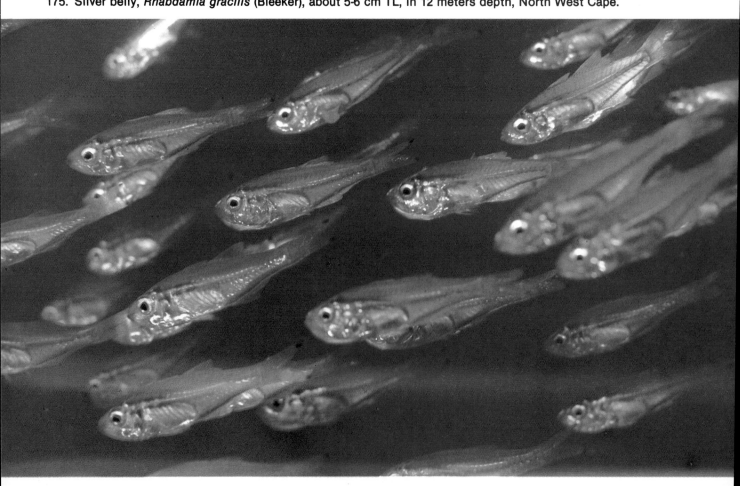

176. Victoria cardinalfish, *Apogon victoriae* (Guenther), about 11 cm TL, in 8 meters depth, Cockburn Sound.

177. Sailfin cardinalfish, *Pterapogon mirifica* (Mees), about 8 cm TL, in 4 meters depth, North West Cape.

178. Southern siphonfish, *Siphamia cephalotes* (Castelnau), 4 cm TL, from 6 meters depth, Rottnest Island.

179. Striped cardinalfish, *Apogon angustatus* (Smith & Radcliffe), 6 cm TL, from 4 meters depth, North West Cape.

180. Spotted cardinalfish, *Vincentia punctatus* (Klunzinger), about 10 cm TL, in 5 meters depth, Point Peron.

181. Many-lined cardinalfish, *Apogon chrysotaenia* Bleeker, about 12 cm TL, in 5 meters depth, North West Cape.

182. Orange stripe cardinalfish, *Apogon* species, about 7 cm TL, in 4 meters depth, Rosemary Island, Dampier Archipelago.

183. Western cardinalfish, *Vincentia* new species, 4.5 cm TL, in 5 meters depth, Garden Island.

184. Trumpeter whiting, *Sillago maculata* Quoy & Gaimard, 9 cm TL, from one meter depth, Cockburn Sound.

185. Tailor, *Pomatomus saltatrix* Linnaeus, 27 cm TL, from 2 meters depth, Cape Naturaliste.

186. Skipjack trevally, *Pseudocaranx dentex* (Bloch and Schneider), about 20 cm TL, in 10 meters depth, Geographe Bay.

187. Golden trevally, *Gnathanodon speciosus* (Forsskal), about 60 cm TL, in 12 meters depth, North West Cape.

188. Blue-spotted trevally, *Caranx bucculentus* Alleyne & Macleay, 25 cm TL, from fish market at Ambon, Indonesia.

189. Jellyfish jack, *Carangoides* species, 5 cm TL, from surface where it was associated with a floating jellyfish, North West Cape.

190. Plumed trevally, *Alectis indicus* (Rueppell), about 15 cm TL, in 10 meters depth, North West Cape.

191. Fringe-finned trevally, *Pantolabus radiatus* (Macleay), 24 cm TL, from 10 meters depth, Port Hedland. Only males have fin ray extensions.

192. Black spotted swallowtail, *Trachinotus baillonii* (Lacepede), about 14 cm TL, in 2 meters depth, Kendrew Island, Dampier Archipelago.

193. Tommy rough, *Arripis georgianus* (Valenciennes), 28 cm TL, from 2 meters depth, no locality.

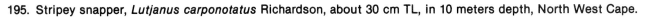

194. Stripey snapper, *Lutjanus carponotatus* Richardson, 10 cm TL, from 2 meters depth, Rosemary Island, Dampier Archipelago.

195. Stripey snapper, *Lutjanus carponotatus* Richardson, about 30 cm TL, in 10 meters depth, North West Cape.

196. Dark tailed snapper, *Lutjanus lemniscatus* (Valenciennes), about 20 cm TL, in 2 meters depth, Kendrew Island, Dampier Archipelago.

197. Black spot snapper, *Lutjanus fulviflammus* Forsskal, about 20 cm TL, in 3 meters depth, Kendrew Island, Dampier Archipelago.

198. Hog snapper, *Lutjanus* species (possibly young of *L. lemniscatus*), 4 cm TL, from 5 meters depth, North West Cape.

199. Double stripe fusilier, *Pterocaesio diagramma* (Bleeker), about 17 cm TL, in 12 meters depth, North West Cape.

200. Black stripe butterfish, *Pentapodus vitta* (Quoy & Gaimard), 17 cm TL, from 3 meters depth, Cockburn Sound.

201. Ornate butterfish, *Pentapodus porosus* (Valenciennes), 18 cm TL, from 3 meters depth, Exmouth Gulf.

202. Black stripe butterfish, *Pentapodus vitta* (Quoy & Gaimard), about 10 cm TL, in 3 meters depth, Rosemary Island, Dampier Archipelago.

203. Double-lined coral bream, *Scolopsis bilineatus* (Bloch), about 15 cm TL, in 6 meters depth, Kendrew Island, Dampier Archipelago.

204. Regal coral bream, *Scolopsis monogramma* (Cuvier), about 30 cm TL, in 10 meters depth, North West Cape.

205. Tarwhine, *Rhabdosargus sarba* (Forsskal), 28 cm TL, from a depth of 5 meters, Port Hedland.

206. Japanese bream, *Mylio latus* (Houttuyn), 26 cm TL, from 5 meters depth, Port Hedland.

207. Gray emperor, *Gymnocranius griseus* (Temminck & Schlegel), 6 cm TL, from 3 meters depth, North West Cape.

208. Variegated emperor, *Lethrinus variegatus* Valenciennes, about 25 cm TL, in 15 meters depth, North West Cape.

209. Silverbelly, *Parequula melbournensis* (Castelnau), about 10 cm TL, in 10 meters depth, Geographe Bay.

210. Flagfin mojarra, *Gerres filamentosus* Cuvier, 8 cm TL, in one meter depth, Maitland River.

211. Dusky sweetlips, *Plectorhynchus nigrus* (Cuvier), 8 cm TL, from one meter depth, Exmouth Gulf.

212. Gold-spotted sweetlips, *Plectorhynchus flavomaculatus* (Cuvier), about 30 cm TL, in 3 meters depth, Lady Nora Island, Dampier Archipelago.

213. Pale sweetlips, *Plectorhynchus pictus* (Thunberg), about 8 cm TL, in 5 meters depth, North West Cape.

214. Blackspot goatfish, *Parupeneus fraterculus* Valenciennes, about 28 cm TL, in 10 meters depth, North West Cape.

215. Blackspot goatfish, *Parupeneus fraterculus* Valenciennes, about 30 cm TL, in 10 meters depth, Houtman Abrolhos.

216. Indian goatfish, *Parupeneus indicus* Shaw, about 22 cm TL, in 10 meters depth, Kendrew Island, Dampier Archipelago.

217. Bar-tailed goatfish, *Upeneus tragula* Richardson, about 16 cm TL, in 10 meters depth, Kendrew Island, Dampier Archipelago.

218. Yellow-striped goatfish, *Parupeneus chrysopleuron* (Schlegel), 7 cm TL, from 40 meters depth, Houtman Abrolhos.

219. Yellow goatfish, *Parupeneus cyclostomus* (Lacepede), about 30 cm TL, in 12 meters depth, Christmas Island, Indian Ocean.

220. Two-banded goatfish, *Parupeneus bifasciatus* (Lacepede), about 30 cm TL, in 10 meters depth, Christmas Island, Indian Ocean.

221. Blue-spotted goatfish, *Upeneichthys lineatus* (Bloch & Schneider), about 30 cm TL, in 15 meters depth, Recherche Archipelago.

222. Rough bullseye, *Pempheris klunzingeri* McCulloch, about 16 cm TL, in 20 meters depth, Geographe Bay.

223. Rough bullseye, *Pempheris klunzingeri* McCulloch, about 12 cm TL, in 6 meters depth, Rottnest Island.

224. Blacktip bullseye, *Pempheris analis* Waite, 12 cm TL, from 8 meters depth, North West Cape.

225. Oualan bullseye, *Pempheris oualensis* Cuvier, about 20 cm TL, in 4 meters depth, North West Cape.

226. Striped bullseye, *Pempheris schwenkii* Bleeker, about 18 cm TL, in 5 meters depth, Kendrew Island, Dampier Archipelago.

227. Oualan bullseye, *Pempheris oualensis* Cuvier, 18 cm TL, from 2 meters depth, Houtman Abrolhos.

228. Striped bullseye, *Pempheris schwenkii* Bleeker, about 20 cm TL, in 5 meters depth, Kendrew Island, Dampier Archipelago.

229. Bullseye, *Pempheris* species, about 6 cm TL, in 5 meters depth, Geographe Bay .

230. Woodward's pomfret, *Schuettea woodwardi* (Waite), about 6 cm TL, in one meter depth, Cape Naturaliste.

231. Slender bullseye, *Parapriacanthus unwini* (Ogilby), 7 cm TL, from 12 meters depth, North West Cape.

232. Slender bullseye, *Parapriacanthus unwini* (Ogilby), about 7 cm TL, in 12 meters depth, North West Cape.

233. Spotted archerfish, *Toxotes chatareus* (Hamilton), 7.5 cm TL, from surface waters of Lake Kununurra.

234. Northern buffalo bream, *Kyphosus gibsoni* (Ogilby), about 20 cm TL, in 3 meters depth, Lady Nora Island, Dampier Archipelago.

235. Common buffalo bream, *Kyphosus sydneyanus* (Guenther), about 15 cm TL, in 2 meters depth, Geographe Bay.

236. Western buffalo bream, *Kyphosus cornelii* (Whitley), 10 cm TL, from one meter depth, Houtman Abrolhos.

237. Common buffalo bream, *Kyphosus sydneyanus* (Guenther), about 80 cm TL, in 5 meters depth, Houtman Abrolhos.

238. Zebrafish, *Girella zebra* (Richardson), about 30 cm TL, in 20 meters depth, Geographe Bay.

239. Zebrafish, *Girella zebra* (Richardson), 7 cm TL, from tidepool at Cape Naturaliste.

240. Western rock blackfish, *Girella tephraeops* (Richardson), 15 cm TL, from tidepool at Cape Naturaliste.

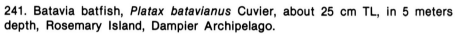

241. Batavia batfish, *Platax batavianus* Cuvier, about 25 cm TL, in 5 meters depth, Rosemary Island, Dampier Archipelago.

242. Spotted spadefish, *Drepane punctata* (Linnaeus), 20 cm TL, from fish market on Ambon Island, Indonesia.

243. Stripey, *Microcanthus strigatus* (Cuvier), about 15 cm TL, in 2 meters depth, Houtman Abrolhos.

244. Banded sweep, *Scorpis georgianus* Valenciennes, about 35 cm TL, in 15 meters depth, Houtman Abrolhos.

245. Sea sweep, *Scorpis aequipinnis* Richardson, about 30 cm TL, in 20 meters depth, Recherche Archipelago.

246. Western footballer, *Neatypus obliquus* Waite, about 14 cm TL, in 10 meters depth, Geographe Bay.

247. Moonlighter, *Tilodon sexfasciatum* (Richardson), about 30 cm TL, in 10 meters depth, Geographe Bay.

248. Truncate coralfish, *Chelmonops truncatus* (Kner), about 5 cm TL, in 8 meters depth, Esperance.

249. Western butterflyfish, *Chaetodon assarius* Waite, about 13 cm TL, in 14 meters depth, Houtman Abrolhos.

250. Ocellate butterflyfish, *Parachaetodon ocellatus* (Cuvier), about 6 cm TL, in 2 meters depth, Houtman Abrolhos.

251. Emperor angelfish, *Pomacanthus imperator* (Bloch), 5 cm TL, from 10 meters depth, North West Cape.

252. Semicircle angelfish, *Pomacanthus semicirculatus* (Cuvier), about 30 cm TL, in 15 meters depth, North West Cape.

253. Semicircle angelfish, *Pomacanthus semicirculatus* (Cuvier), 5 cm TL, from 4 meters depth, North West Cape.

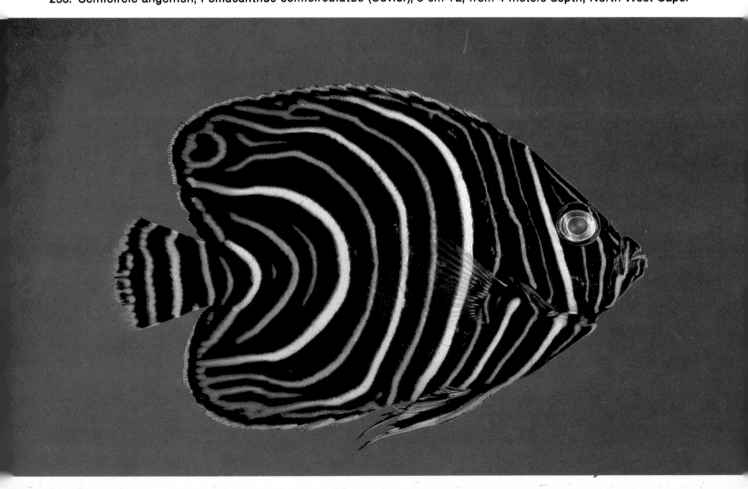

254. Yellowtail angelfish, *Chaetodontoplus personifer* (McCulloch), about 14 cm TL, in 15 meters depth, North West Cape.

255. Scribbled angelfish, *Chaetodontoplus duboulayi* (Guenther), about 16 cm TL, in 15 meters depth, North West Cape.

256. Three-spot angelfish, *Apolemichthys trimaculatus* (Cuvier), 20 cm TL, from 15 meters depth, North West Cape.

257. Blue-girdled angelfish, *Euxiphipops navarchus* (Cuvier), about 20 cm TL, in 8 meters depth, Rowley Shoals.

258. Eibl's angelfish, *Centropyge eibli* Klausewitz, about 12 cm TL, in 18 meters depth, Christmas Island, Indian Ocean.

259. Old wife, *Enoplosus armatus* (White), about 22 cm TL, in 10 meters depth, Recherche Archipelago.

260. Long-snouted boarfish, *Pentaceropsis recurvirostris* (Richardson), about 70 cm TL, in 10 meters depth, Geographe Bay.

261. Bengal sergeant, *Abudefduf bengalensis* (Bloch), about 15 cm TL, in 5 meters depth, Houtman Abrolhos.

262. Northwest anemonefish, *Amphiprion rubrocinctus* Richardson, 3 cm TL, from 5 meters depth, Rosemary Island, Dampier Archipelago.

263. Northwest anemonefish, *Amphiprion rubrocinctus* Richardson, 7 cm TL, from 5 meters depth, Rosemary Island, Dampier Archipelago.

264. Miller's damselfish, *Pomacentrus milleri* Taylor, about 7 cm TL, in 10 meters depth, Kendrew Island, Dampier Archipelago.

265. Miller's damselfish, *Pomacentrus milleri* Taylor, about 3 cm TL, in 8 meters depth, Kendrew Island, Dampier Archipelago.

266. Western gregory, *Stegastes obreptus* (Whitley), about 12 cm TL, in 8 meters depth, Kendrew Island, Dampier Archipelago.

267. Brown demoiselle, *Neopomacentrus filamentosus* (Macleay), 7 cm TL, from 6 meters depth, Rosemary Island, Dampier Archipelago.

268. Black-headed puller, *Chromis klunzingeri* Whitley, about 8 cm TL, in 20 meters depth, Recherche Archipelago.

269. Fawn chromis, *Chromis fumea* (Tanaka), about 3 cm TL, in 10 meters depth, Rosemary Island, Dampier Archipelago.

270. Westralian puller, *Chromis westaustralis* Allen, about 5 cm TL, in 15 meters depth, Houtman Abrolhos.

271. Westralian puller, *Chromis westaustralis* Allen, about 7 cm TL, in 10 meters depth, Houtman Abrolhos.

272. Peppered chromis, *Chromis cinerascens* (Cuvier), 10 cm TL, from 10 meters depth, Kendrew Island, Dampier Archipelago. Photo by Dr. John E. Randall.

273. Banded damsel, *Dischistodus fasciatus* (Cuvier), about 5 cm TL, in 8 meters depth, Rosemary Island, Dampier Archipelago.

274. Western scalyfin, *Parma occidentalis* Allen & Hoese, about 30 cm TL, in 10 meters depth, Houtman Abrolhos.

275. Western scalyfin, *Parma occidentalis* Allen & Hoese, about 7.5 cm TL, in 8 meters depth, Houtman Abrolhos.

276. McCulloch's scalyfin, *Parma mccullochi* Whitley, about 10 cm TL, in 10 meters depth, Rottnest Island.

277. McCulloch's scalyfin, *Parma mccullochi* Whitley, about 5 cm TL, in 8 meters depth, Geographe Bay.

278. Bicolor scalyfin, *Parma bicolor* Allen & Larson, about 18 cm TL, in 15 meters depth, Recherche Archipelago.

279. Victorian scalyfin, *Parma victoriae* (Guenther), about 20 cm TL, in 10 meters depth, Recherche Archipelago.

280. Red barred hawkfish, *Cirrhitichthys aprinus* (Cuvier), 7 cm TL, from 30 meters depth, Houtman Abrolhos.

281. Lyretail hawkfish, *Cyprinocirrhites polyactis* (Bleeker), 7 cm TL, from 132 meters depth, Barrow Island.

282. Spotted hawkfish, *Cirrhitichthys oxycephalus* (Bleeker), about 8 cm TL, in 15 meters depth, Christmas Island, Indian Ocean.

283. Spotted hawkfish, *Cirrhitichthys oxycephalus* (Bleeker), about 8 cm TL, in 12 meters depth, North West Cape.

284. Arc-eyed hawkfish, *Paracirrhites arcatus* (Cuvier), about 10 cm TL, in 16 meters depth, Christmas Island, Indian Ocean.

285. Silver spot, *Threpterius maculosus* Richardson, about 12 cm TL, in 4 meters depth, Point Peron.

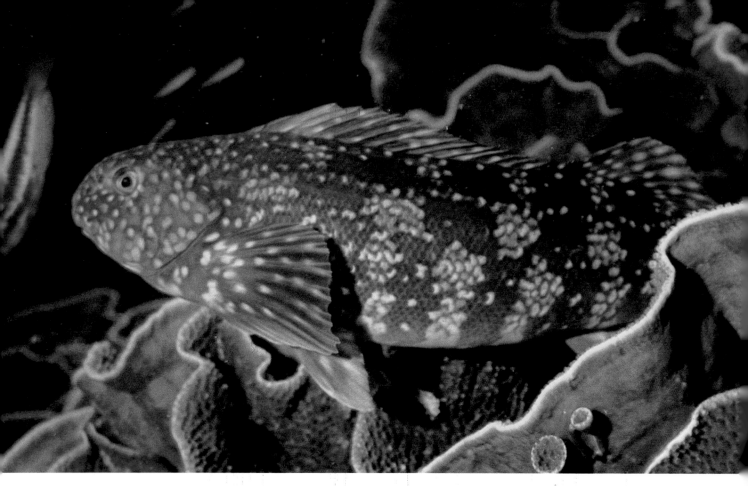

286. Sea carp, *Dactylosargus* species, about 80 cm TL, in 10 meters depth, Recherche Archipelago.

287. Dusky morwong, *Dactylophora nigricans* (Richardson), about 100 cm TL, in 12 meters depth, Recherche Archipelago.

288. Red lip morwong, *Cheilodactylus rubrolabiatus* Allen & Heemstra, about 35 cm TL, in 10 meters depth, Houtman Abrolhos.

289. Red lip morwong, *Cheilodactylus rubrolabiatus* Allen & Heemstra, 4 cm TL, from one meter depth, Albany.

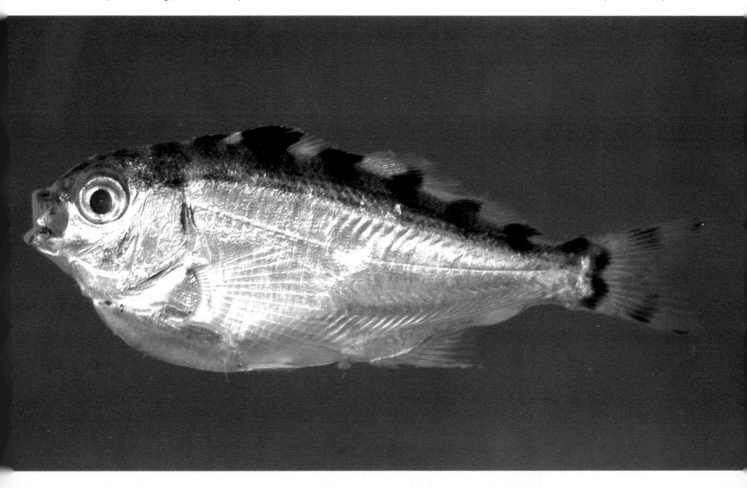

290. Crested morwong, *Cheilodactylus gibbosus* Richardson, about 12 cm TL, in 4 meters depth, Geographe Bay.

291. Crested morwong, *Cheilodactylus gibbosus* Richardson, about 12 cm TL, in 4 meters depth, Geographe Bay.

292. Magpie morwong, *Cheilodactylus nigripes* Richardson, 10 cm TL, from rock pool at Kiama, New South Wales. Photo by Rudie Kuiter.

293. Blue morwong, *Nemadactylus valenciennesi* (Whitley), about 25 cm TL, in 6 meters depth, Recherche Archipelago.

294. Diamond scale mullet, *Liza vaigiensis* (Quoy & Gaimard), 30 cm TL, from 2 meters depth, Rosemary Island, Dampier Archipelago.

295. Diamond scale mullet, *Liza vaigiensis* (Quoy & Gaimard), 8 cm TL, from one meter depth, Rosemary Island, Dampier Archipelago.

296. Yelloweye mullet, *Aldrichetta forsteri* (Valenciennes), 12 cm TL, from one meter depth, Houtman Abrolhos.

297. Striped seapike, *Sphyraena obtusata* Cuvier, about 20 cm TL, in 10 meters depth, Houtman Abrolhos.

298. Ornate wrasse, *Dotalabrus aurantiacus* (Castelnau), about 10 cm TL, in 10 meters depth, Geographe Bay.

299. Red-banded wrasse, *Pseudolabrus biserialis* (Klunzinger), female about 12 cm TL, in 20 meters depth, Rottnest Island.

300. Red-banded wrasse, *Pseudolabrus biserialis* (Klunzinger), male about 20 cm TL, in 20 meters depth, Recherche Archipelago.

301. Brown spotted wrasse, *Pseudolabrus parilus* (Richardson), male about 38 cm TL, in 15 meters depth, Rottnest Island.

302. Brown spotted wrasse, *Pseudolabrus parilus* (Richardson), female about 20 cm TL, in 20 meters depth, Recherche Archipelago.

303. Red back wrasse, *Suezichthys* species, 5 cm TL, from 20 meters depth, Houtman Abrolhos.

304. Rainbow wrasse, *Dotalabrus* species, female 7 cm TL, from 3 meters depth, Rottnest Island.

305. Rainbow wrasse, *Dotalabrus* species, male 9 cm TL, from 3 meters depth, Rottnest Island.

306. Senator wrasse, *Pictilabrus laticlavius* (Richardson), 18 cm TL, from 8 meters depth, Carnac Island.

307. Senator wrasse, *Pictilabrus laticlavius* (Richardson), about 8 cm TL, in 10 meters depth, Geographe Bay.

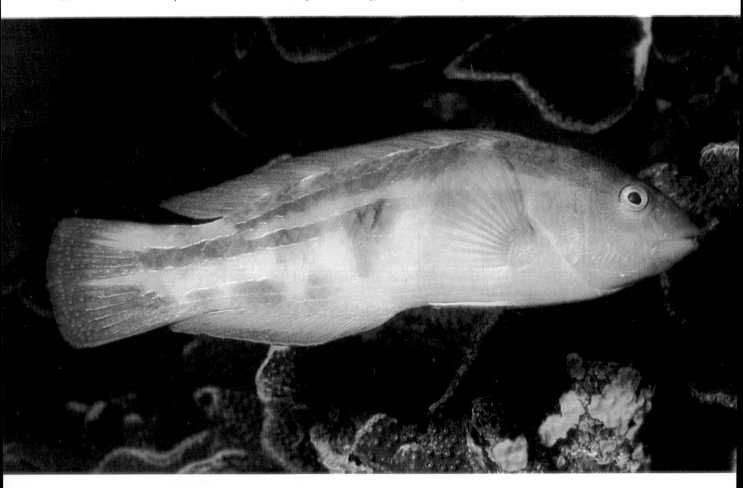

308. False senator wrasse, *Pictilabrus* sp. (undescribed), 14 cm TL, from 4 meters depth, Geographe Bay.

309. Black-spotted wrasse, *Austrolabrus maculatus* (Macleay), about 12 cm TL, in 20 meters depth, Rottnest Island.

310. Slender wrasse, *Eupetrichthys angustipes* Ramsay & Ogilby, about 12 cm TL, in 8 meters depth, Esperance.

311. Blue grouper, *Achoerodus gouldii* (Richardson), about 90 cm TL, in 15 meters depth, Recherche Archipelago.

312. Maori wrasse, *Ophthalmolepis lineolatus* (Valenciennes), male about 35 cm TL, in 8 meters depth, Geographe Bay.

313. Maori wrasse, *Ophthalmolepis lineolatus* (Valenciennes), female about 20 cm TL, in 7 meters depth, Garden Island.

314. King wrasse, *Coris auricularis* (Valenciennes), male about 35 cm TL, in 15 meters depth, Houtman Abrolhos.

315. King wrasse, *Coris auricularis* (Valenciennes), female about 25 cm TL, in 10 meters depth, Garden Island.

316. King wrasse, *Coris auricularis* (Valenciennes), juvenile about 8 cm TL, in 8 meters depth, Houtman Abrolhos.

317. Spotted tail wrasse, *Coris caudimacula* Quoy & Gaimard, 12 cm TL, from 10 meters depth, North West Cape.

318. Spotted tail wrasse, *Coris caudimacula* Quoy & Gaimard, about 14 cm TL, in 12 meters depth, North West Cape.

319. Spotted tail wrasse, *Coris pictoides* Randall & Kuiter, 5 cm TL, from 20 meters depth, Dampier Archipelago.

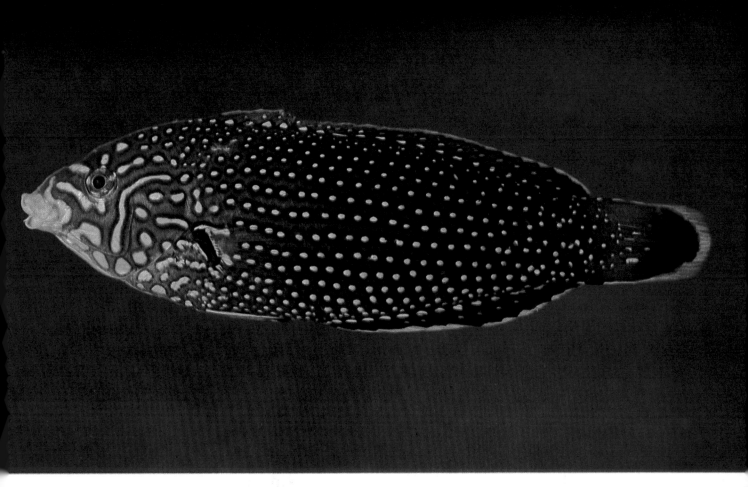

320. Blue spot wrasse, *Anampses caeruleopunctatus* Rueppell, 8 cm TL, from 4 meters depth, North West Cape.

321. Yellowtail wrasse, *Anampses meleagrides* Valenciennes, 9 cm TL, from 6 meters depth, North West Cape.

322. Lennard's wrasse, *Anampses lennardi* Scott, female about 25 cm TL, in 5 meters depth, Rosemary Island, Dampier Archipelago.

323. Lennard's wrasse, *Anampses lennardi* Scott, 5 cm TL, from 3 meters depth, Rosemary Island, Dampier Archipelago.

324. Saddleback wrasse, *Bodianus bilunulatus* (Lacepede), about 30 cm TL, in 12 meters depth, Houtman Abrolhos.

325. Saddleback wrasse, *Bodianus bilunulatus* (Lacepede), 5 cm TL, from 12 meters depth, North West Cape.

326. Foxfish, *Bodianus frenchii* (Klunzinger), about 30 cm TL, in 15 meters depth, Recherche Archipelago.

327. White spot tuskfish, *Choerodon cyanodus* (Richardson), about 30 cm TL, in 2 meters depth, Kendrew Island, Dampier Archipelago.

328. Baldchin tuskfish, *Choerodon rubescens* (Guenther), about 38 cm TL, in 10 meters depth, Houtman Abrolhos.

329. Baldchin tuskfish, *Choerodon rubescens* (Guenther), about 75 cm TL, in 10 meters depth, Houtman Abrolhos.

330. Blue spot tuskfish, *Choerodon* species, 5 cm TL, from 3 meters depth, Rosemary Island, Dampier Archipelago.

331. Blue spot tuskfish, *Choerodon* species, about 30 cm TL, in 15 meters depth, North West Cape.

332. Jordan's tuskfish, *Choerodon jordani* (Snyder), 9 cm TL, from 30 meters depth, Houtman Abrolhos.

333. Red stripe tuskfish, *Choerodon vitta* Ogilby, 24 cm TL, from 20 meters depth, Monte Bello Island.

334. Short tail tuskfish, *Choerodon* species, 21 cm TL, from 20 meters depth, Monte Bello Island

335. Peacock wrasse, *Cirrhilabrus temmincki* Bleeker, male about 10 cm TL, from 12 meters depth, North West Cape.

336. Peacock wrasse, *Cirrhilabrus temmincki* Bleeker, male about 9 cm TL, from 30 meters depth, Houtman Abrolhos.

337. Peacock wrasse, *Cirrhilabrus temmincki* Bleeker, female 7 cm TL, from 30 meters depth, Houtman Abrolhos.

338. Flagfin wrasse, *Pteragogus flagellifera* (Valenciennes), 14 cm TL, from 4 meters depth, Exmouth Gulf.

339. Double spot wrasse, *Halichoeres bimaculatus* Rueppell, 12 cm TL, from 8 meters depth, Kendrew Island, Dampier Archipelago.

340. Marginate wrasse, *Halichoeres marginatus* Rueppell, male about 15 cm TL, in 5 meters depth, Kendrew Island, Dampier Archipelago.

341. Marginate wrasse, *Halichoeres marginatus* Rueppell, about 4 cm TL, in 2 meters depth, Kendrew Island, Dampier Archipelago.

342. Diamond wrasse, *Halichoeres nigrescens* Bleeker, 14 cm TL, from one meter depth, Rosemary Island, Dampier Archipelago.

343. Brownfield's wrasse, *Halichoeres brownfieldi* (Whitley), male 12 cm TL, from 4 meters depth, Geographe Bay.

344. Purple wrasse, *Halichoeres melanochir* Fowler & Bean, 5 cm TL, from 10 meters depth, Rosemary Island, Dampier Archipelago.

345. Red-lined wrasse, *Halichoeres biocellatus* Schultz, about 18 cm TL, in 5 meters depth, Christmas Island, Indian Ocean.

346. Red-lined wrasse, *Halichoeres biocellatus* Schultz, 12 cm TL, from 10 meters depth, North West Cape.

347. Carpet wrasse, *Novaculichthys taeniorus* (Lacepede), 10 cm TL, from 5 meters depth, Rosemary Island, Dampier Archipelago.

348. Banda wrasse, *Stethojulis bandanensis* (Bleeker), female, 9 cm TL, from 3 meters depth, Rottnest Island.

349. Seven banded wrasse, *Thalassoma septemfasciata* Scott, female, 20 cm TL, from one meter depth, Houtman Abrolhos.

350. Blue-fin wrasse, *Thalassoma lutescens* (Lay & Bennett), male about 30 cm TL, in 5 meters depth, Christmas Island, Indian Ocean.

351. Pink speckled wrasse, *Xenojulis margaritaceous* (Macleay), 12 cm TL, from 5 meters depth, Kendrew Island, Dampier Archipelago.

352. Elongate wrasse, *Pseudojuloides elongatus* Ayling & Russell, male, about 14 cm TL, from 5 meters depth, North West Cape.

353. Elongate wrasse, *Pseudojuloides elongatus* Ayling & Russell, female, 10 cm TL, from 4 meters depth, North West Cape.

354. Herring cale, *Odax cyanomelas* (Richardson), 5 cm TL, from 3 meters depth, Geographe Bay.

355. Herring cale, *Odax cyanomelas* (Richardson), 15 cm TL, from 5 meters depth, Rottnest Island.

356. Sharp-nosed weed whiting, *Siphonognathus caninus* Scott , 9 cm TL, from 10 meters depth, Rottnest Island.

357. Sharp-nosed weed whiting, *Siphonognathus caninus* Scott , 7 cm TL, from 20 meters depth, off Point Peron.

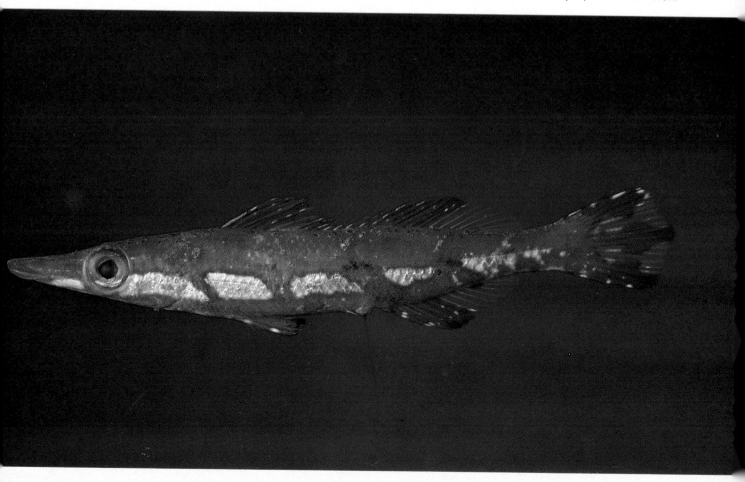

358. Sharp-nosed weed whiting, *Siphonognathus caninus* Scott , 5 cm TL, from 8 meters depth, Rottnest Island.

359. Little weed whiting, *Neoodax balteatus* (Valenciennes), 7 cm TL, from 4 meters depth, Cockburn Sound.

360. Bridled weed whiting, *Siphonognathus radiatus* (Quoy & Gaimard), 12 cm TL, from 4 meters depth, Cockburn Sound.

361. Bridled weed whiting, *Siphonognathus radiatus* (Quoy & Gaimard), 12 cm TL, from 4 meters depth, Cockburn Sound.

362. Slender weed whiting, *Siphonognathus beddomei* (Johnson), 10 cm TL, from 8 meters depth, Carnac Island.

363. Tubemouth, *Siphonognathus argyrophanes* Richardson, 30 cm TL, from 5 meters depth, Rottnest Island.

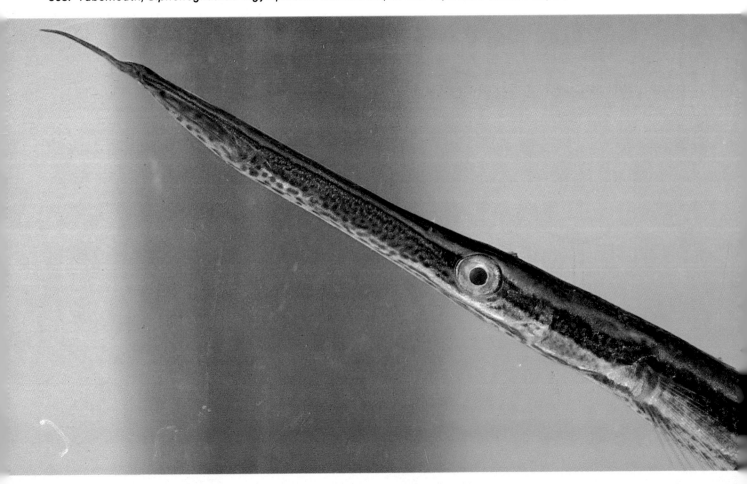

364. Blue-barred parrotfish, *Scarus ghobban* Forsskal, female, about 30 cm TL, in 3 meters depth, Kendrew Island, Dampier Archipelago.

365. Parrotfish, *Scarus* species, 4 cm TL, from 4 meters depth, North West Cape.

366. Rainbowfish, *Odax acroptilus* (Richardson), female, 12 cm TL, from 6 meters depth, Carnac Island.

367. Rainbowfish, *Odax acroptilus* (Richardson), male, 16 cm TL, from 10 meters depth, Houtman Abrolhos.

368. Rainbowfish, *Odax acroptilus* (Richardson), male, about 16 cm TL, in 10 meters depth, Geographe Bay.

369. Darwin jawfish, *Opistognathus darwiniensis* Macleay, 23 cm TL, from 3 meters depth, Rosemary Island, Dampier Archipelago.

370. Wavy grubfish, *Parapercis haackei* (Steindachner), about 12 cm TL, in 10 meters depth, Geographe Bay.

371. Spot head grubfish, *Parapercis cephalopunctata* (Seale), 6 cm TL, from 8 meters depth, North West Cape.

372. Red banded grubfish, *Parapercis* species, 7 cm TL, from 20 meters depth, North West Cape.

373. Sand lance, *Trichonotus setiger* Bloch & Schneider, 18 cm TL, from 7 meters depth, Kendrew Island, Dampier Archipelago.

374. Tommyfish, *Limnichthys fasciatus* Waite, 3 cm TL, from 5 meters depth, Garden Island.

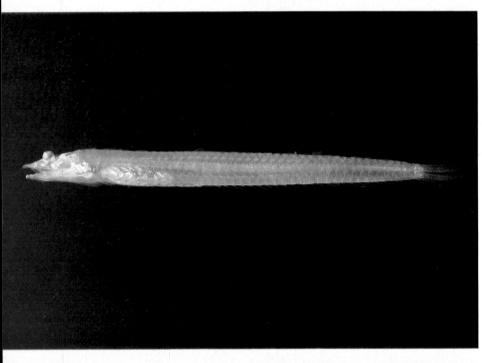

375. Slender sandfish, *Creedia alleni* Nelson, 5 cm TL, from 20 meters depth, off Point Peron.

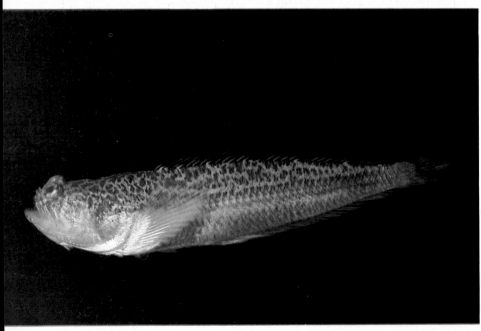

376. Sandfish, *Crapatalus arenarius* McCulloch, 6.5 cm TL, from 30 meters depth, off Point Peron.

377. Black blenny, *Atrosalarias fuscus holomelas* (Guenther), 4 cm TL, from 3 meters depth, Houtman Abrolhos.

378. Dusky blenny, *Cirripectes filamentosus* (Alleyne & Macleay), about 7 cm TL, in 4 meters depth, Kendrew Island, Dampier Archipelago.

379. Coral blenny, *Ecsenius yaeyamaensis* (Aoyagi), 5 cm TL, from 5 meters depth, North West Cape.

380. Lined blenny, *Ecsenius lineatus* Klausewitz, 6 cm TL, from 12 meters depth, North West Cape.

381. Bicolor blenny, *Ecsenius bicolor* (Day) (dark phase), about 7 cm TL, in 5 meters depth, Kendrew Island, Dampier Archipelago.

382. Bicolor blenny, *Ecsenius bicolor* (Day) (bicolor phase), about 7 cm TL, in 8 meters depth, Kendrew Island, Dampier Archipelago.

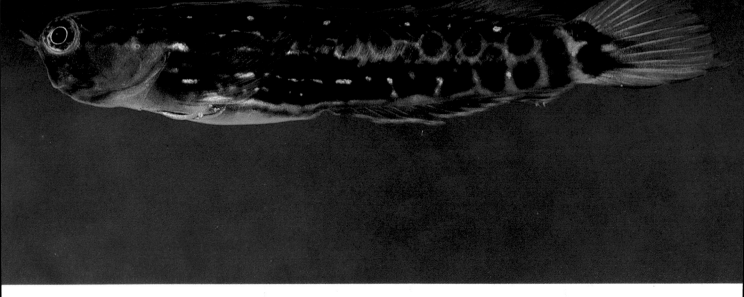

383. Ocular blenny, *Ecsenius oculus* Springer, 5 cm TL, from 4 meters depth, North West Cape.

384. Wavy lined blenny, *Entomacrodus decussatus* (Bleeker), about 10 cm TL, in one meter depth, Kendrew Island, Dampier Archipelago.

385. Striated blenny, *Entomacrodus striatus* (Quoy & Gaimard), about 7 cm TL, in one meter depth, Kendrew Island, Dampier Archipelago.

386. Leopard blenny, *Exallias brevis* (Kner), about 15 cm TL, in 10 meters depth, Christmas Island, Indian Ocean.

387. Red spotted blenny, *Istiblennius chrysospilos* (Bleeker), about 10 cm TL, in one meter depth, Kendrew Island, Dampier Archipelago.

388. Schultz' triplefin, *Norfolkia brachylepis* (Schultz), 3.5 cm TL, from 8 meters depth, Garden Island.

389. Edentulate blenny, *Istiblennius edentulus* (Bloch & Schneider), male about 12 cm TL, in one meter depth, Kendrew Island, Dampier Archipelago.

390. Edentulate blenny, *Istiblennius edentulus* (Bloch & Schneider), female about 12 cm TL, in one meter depth, Kendrew Island, Dampier Archipelago.

391. Tide pool blenny, *Istiblennius lineatus* (Valenciennes), about 12 cm TL, in one meter depth, Kendrew Island, Dampier Archipelago.

392. Spotted blenny, *Istiblennius meleagris* (Valenciennes), about 8 cm TL, in one meter depth, Kendrew Island, Dampier Archipelago.

393. Rock blenny, *Istiblennius periophthalmus* (Valenciennes), about 12 cm TL, in one meter depth, Kendrew Island, Dampier Archipelago.

394. Many spotted blenny, *Laiphognathus multimaculatus* Smith, about 4 cm TL, in 2 meters depth, Rosemary Island, Dampier Archipelago.

395. Germain's blenny, *Omobranchus germaini* (Sauvage), 7 cm TL, from one meter depth, Cockburn Sound.

396. Rotund blenny, *Omobranchus ferox* (Herre), 5 cm TL, from one meter depth, West Lewis Island, Dampier Archipelago.

397. Weed blenny, *Petroscirtes breviceps* Valenciennes, 5 cm TL, from 2 meters depth, Rosemary Island, Dampier Archipelago.

398. Miter blenny, *Petroscirtes mitratus* Rueppell, 4 cm TL, from 2 meters depth, Houtman Abrolhos.

399. False Tasmanian blenny, *Parablennius* species, 5 cm TL, from 2 meters depth, Cockburn Sound.

400. Sabretooth blenny, *Plagiotremus tapeinosoma* (Klunzinger), about 10 cm TL, in 10 meters depth, North West Cape.

401. Banded blenny, *Salarias fasciatus* (Bloch), about 10 cm TL, in 2 meters depth, Kendrew Island, Dampier Archipelago.

402. Starry blenny, *Salarias* species, about 10 cm TL, from 4 meters depth, North West Cape.

403. Talbot's blenny, *Stanulus talboti* Springer, 5 cm TL, from 3 meters depth, North West Cape.

404. Carpet eel blenny, *Congrogadus subducens* Richardson, about 4 cm TL, from 2 meters depth, Rosemary Island, Dampier Archipelago.

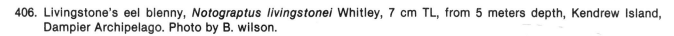

405. Ocellate eel blenny, *Blennodesmus scapularis* Guenther, about 5 cm TL, in 3 meters depth, Kendrew Island, Dampier Archipelago.

406. Livingstone's eel blenny, *Notograptus livingstonei* Whitley, 7 cm TL, from 5 meters depth, Kendrew Island, Dampier Archipelago. Photo by B. wilson.

407. Dark backed snake blenny, *Ophiclinus gracilis* Waite, 6 cm TL, from one meter depth, Geographe Bay.

408. Multicolor snake blenny, *Sticharium dorsale* (Guenther), 5 cm TL, from one meter depth, Geographe Bay.

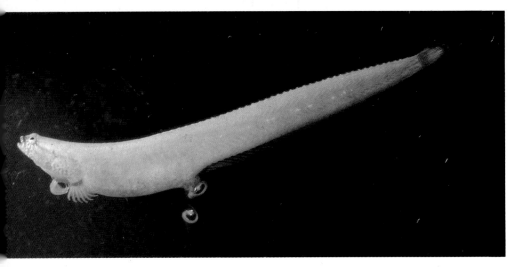

409. Multicolor snake blenny, *Sticharium dorsale* (Guenther), female bearing young, 5 cm TL, from one meter depth, Geographe Bay.

410. Multicolor snake blenny, *Sticharium dorsale* (Guenther), 5 cm TL, from one meter depth, Geographe Bay.

411. Black-throated threefin, *Helcogramma decurrens* McCulloch & Waite, male, 5 cm TL, from 3 meters depth, Geographe Bay.

412. Black-throated threefin, *Helcogramma decurrens* McCulloch & Waite, female, 4 cm TL, from 2 meters depth, Cockburn Sound.

413. Jumping blenny, *Lepidoblennius marmoratus* (Macleay), 9 cm TL, from one meter depth, Geographe Bay.

414. Neon triplefin, *Helcogramma* species, about 3 cm TL, in 5 meters depth, Kendrew Island, Dampier Archipelago.

415. Norwest triplefin, *Norfolkia* species, 5 cm TL, from 3 meters depth, North West Cape.

416. Dampier triplefin, *Norfolkia* species, about 3 cm TL, in 3 meters depth, Kendrew Island, Dampier Archipelago.

417. Abrolhos triplefin, *Vauclusella* species, about 3 cm TL, in 2 meters depth, Houtman Abrolhos.

418. Green triplefin, *Vauclusella* species, about 3 cm TL, in 2 meters depth, Houtman Abrolhos.

419. Rosy triplefin, *Norfolkia* species, about 3 cm TL, in 3 meters depth, Houtman Abrolhos.

420. Weedfish, *Heteroclinus eckloniae* (McKay), 3 cm TL, from 3 meters depth, Geographe Bay.

421. Common weedfish, *Heteroclinus heptaeolus* (Ogilby), 7 cm TL, from 3 meters depth, Geographe Bay.

422. Pink weedfish, *Heteroclinus roseus* (Guenther), 7 cm TL, from 3 meters depth, Geographe Bay.

423. Adelaide weedfish, *Heteroclinus adelaidae* Castelnau, male, 7 cm TL, from 4 meters depth, Cockburn sound.

424. Adelaide Weedfish, *Heteroclinus adelaidae* Castelnau, female, 6 cm TL, from 4 meters depth, Cockburn Sound.

425. Weedfish, *Heteroclinus* species, 8.5 cm TL, from 8 meters depth, Geographe Bay.

426. Whitley's weedfish, *Heteroclinus* species, 6 cm TL, from 8 meters depth, Geographe Bay.

427. Crested weedfish, *Cristiceps australis* Valenciennes, 10 cm TL, from 3 meters depth, Cockburn Sound.

428. Yellow crested weedfish, *Cristiceps aurantiacus* Castelnau, 3.5 cm TL, from 6 meters depth, Geographe Bay.

429. Slender snake blenny, *Ophiclinus pectoralis* George & Springer, 6 cm TL, from 8 meters depth, Geographe Bay.

430. Fingered dragonet, *Dactylopus dactylopus* (Valenciennes), 18 cm TL, from 10 meters depth, Shark Bay.

431. Northern dragonet, *Diplogrammus xenicus* (Jordan & Thompson), 7 cm TL, from 6 meters depth, Kendrew Island, Dampier Archipelago.

432. Goodlad's dragonet, *Callionymus goodladi* (Whitley), 14 cm TL, from 10 meters depth, Cockburn Sound.

433. Northern dragonet, *Diplogrammus xenicus* (Jordan & Thompson), 6 cm TL, from 2 meters depth, Rosemary Island, Dampier Archipelago.

434. Sand dragonet, *Callionymus calcaratus* Macleay, 7 cm TL, from 2 meters depth, Houtman Abrolhos.

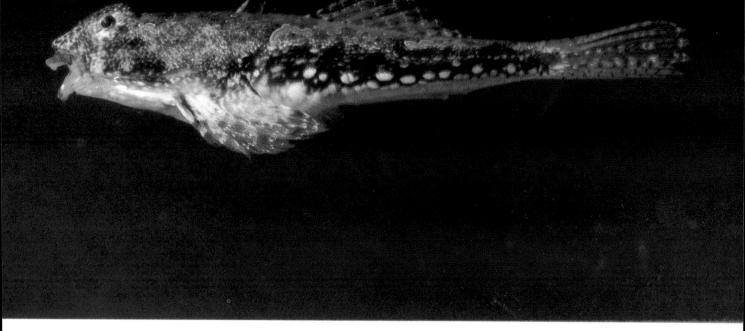

435. Butterfly dragonet, *Synchiropus papilio* Guenther, 4 cm TL, from 10 meters depth, Garden Island.

436. Butterfly dragonet, *Synchiropus papilio* Guenther, 4 cm TL, from 10 meters depth, Garden Island.

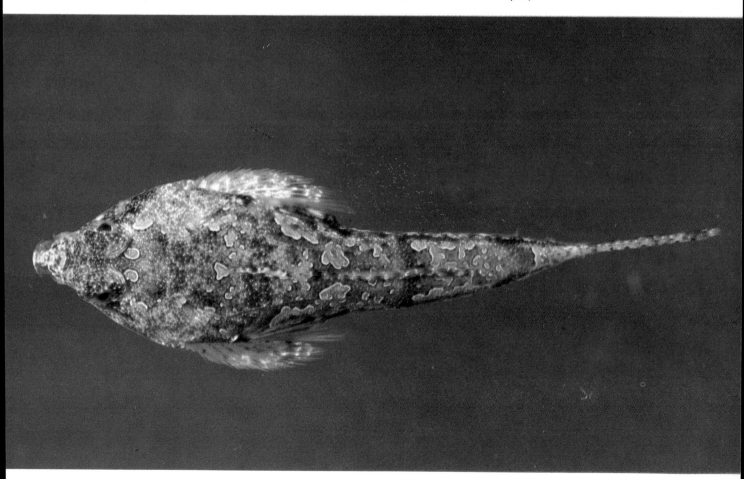

437. Wheeler's shrimp goby, *Amblyeleotris wheeleri* , 6 cm TL, from 10 meters depth, North West Cape.

438. Blue finned shrimp goby, *Cryptocentrus fasciatus* (Playfair), 8 cm TL, from 3 meters depth, Rosemary Island, Dampier Archipelago.

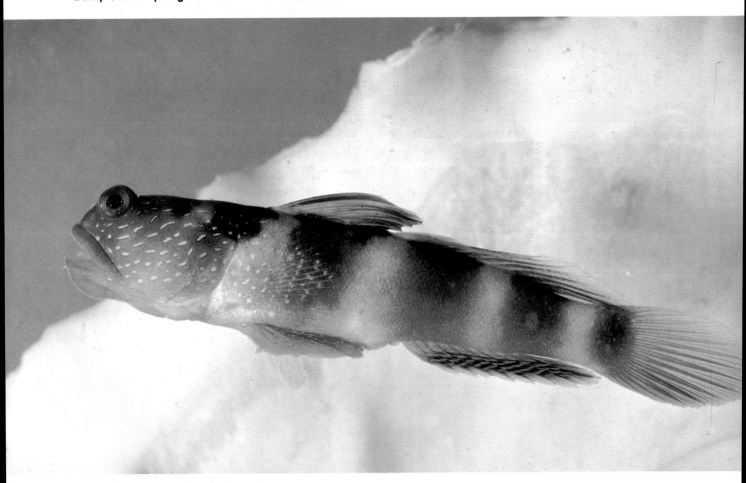

439. Slender shrimp goby, *Amblyeleotris periophthalmus* (Bleeker), 5 cm TL, from 10 meters depth, Kendrew Island, Dampier Archipelago.

440. Green shrimp goby, *Cryptocentrus caeruleomaculatus* (Herre), 5 cm TL, from 2 meters depth, Rosemary Island, Dampier Archipelago.

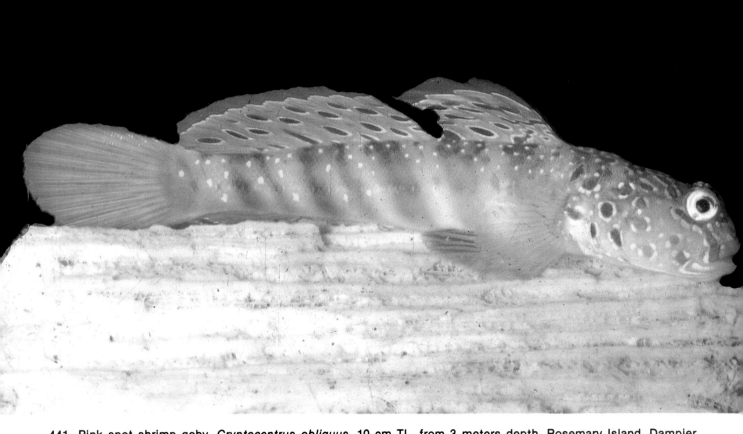

441. Pink spot shrimp goby, *Cryptocentrus obliquus*, 10 cm TL, from 3 meters depth, Rosemary Island, Dampier Archipelago.

442. Pink spot shrimp goby, *Cryptocentrus obliquus,* 10 cm TL, from 3 meters depth, Rosemary Island, Dampier Archipelago.

443. Green coral goby, *Eviota* species, 3 cm TL, from 5 meters depth, Houtman Abrolhos.

444. Sponge goby, *Eviota* species, 3 cm TL, from 15 meters depth, North West Cape.

445. Red coral goby, *Eviota* species, 2 cm TL, from 15 meters depth, Houtman abrolhos.

446. Blue coral goby, *Eviota* species, 2 cm TL, from 10 meters depth, North West Cape.

447. Smith's coral goby, *Eviota infulata* (Smith), 2 cm TL, from 5 meters depth, Houtman Abrolhos.

448. Banded goby, *Amblygobius phalaena* (Valenciennes), about 10 cm TL, in 4 meters depth, Houtman Abrolhos.

449. Pygmy goby, *Pandaka lidwilli* (McCulloch), 1 cm TL, from one meter depth, West Lewis Island, Dampier Archipelago.

450. Starry goby, *Asterropteryx semipunctatus* (Rueppell), 4 cm TL, from 5 meters depth, Houtman Abrolhos.

451. Girdled goby, *Priolepis cinctus* (Regan), 5 cm TL, from 10 meters depth, North West Cape.

452. Orange spot goby, *Trimma okinawae*, 3 cm TL, from 8 meters depth, North West Cape.

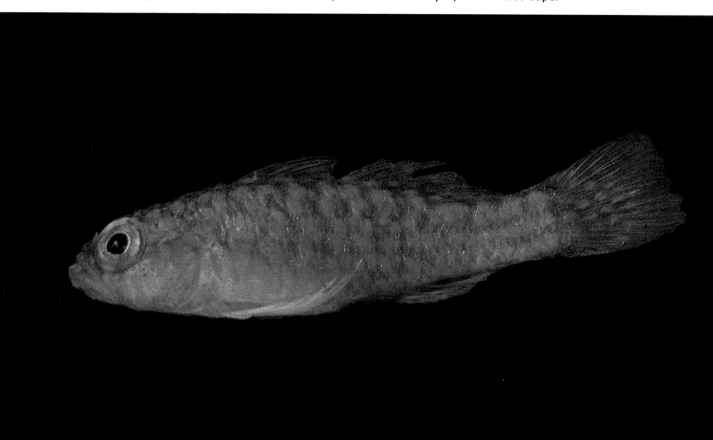

453. Mottled goby, *Trimma* species, 3 cm TL, from 8 meters depth, North West Cape.

454. Redhead goby, *Priolepis semidoliatus* (Valenciennes), 3 cm TL from 20 meters depth, Houtman Abrolhos.

455. Schooling goby, *Parioglossus taeniatus* Regan, 4 cm TL, from 2 meters depth, Rosemary Island, Dampier Archipelago.

456. Schooling goby, *Parioglossus taeniatus* Regan, about 4 cm TL, in 2 meters depth, Lady Nora Island, Dampier Archipelago.

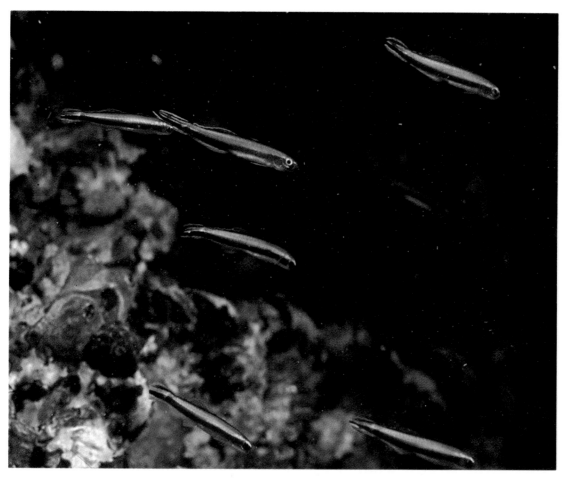

457. Ocellate goby, *Vanderhorstia ornatissimus* Smith, 7 cm TL, from 10 meters depth, Houtman Abrolhos.

458. Blue goby, *Vireosa hanae* Jordan & Snyder, 8 cm TL, from 3 meters depth, Rosemary Island, Dampier Archipelago.

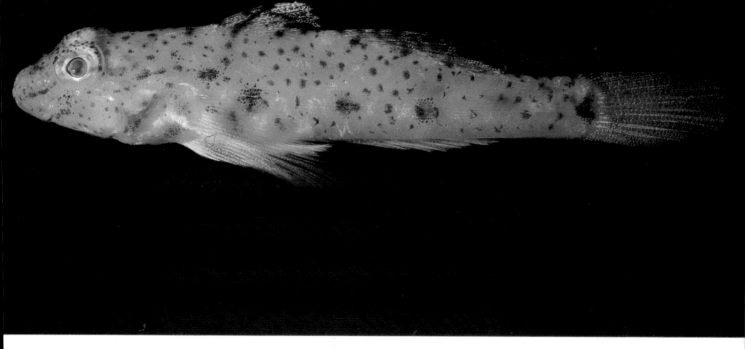

459. Sand goby, *Fusigobius* species, 5 cm TL, from 8 meters depth, North West Cape.

460. Cave goby, *Fusigobius* species, 5 cm TL, from 8 meters depth, North West Cape.

461. Long finned goby, *Favonigobius lateralis* (Macleay), 6 cm TL, from 2 meters depth, Cockburn Sound.

462. Mangrove goby, *Acentrogobius gracilis*, 6 cm TL, from one meter depth, West Lewis Island, Dampier Archipelago.

463. Eleotrid, genus and species undetermined, 4 cm TL, from 5 meters depth, North West Cape.

464. White goby, *Nesogobius* species, 5 cm TL, from 5 meters depth, Rottnest Island.

465. Common goby, *Bathygobius fuscus* (Rueppell), 6 cm TL, from one meter depth, Houtman Abrolhos.

466. Mudskipper, *Periophthalmus regius* Whitley, 8 cm TL, from one meter depth, West Lewis Island, Dampier Archipelago.

467. Orange dashed goby, *Valenciennea puellaris* (Tomiyama), about 12 cm TL, in 2 meters depth, Rosemary Island, Dampier Archipelago.

468. Striped goby, *Valenciennea muralis* (Valenciennes), about 10 cm TL, in 2 meters depth, Kendrew Island, Dampier Archipelago.

469. Orange ear goby, *Gnatholepis inconsequens* Whitley, 6 cm TL, from 20 meters depth, Houtman Abrolhos.

470. Reticulated goby, *Istigobius spence* (Smith), about 7 cm TL, in 2 meters depth, Lady Nora Island, Dampier Archipelago.

471. Ornate goby, *Istigobius ornatus* (Rueppell), about 5 cm TL, in one meter depth, Kendrew Island, Dampier Archipelago.

472. Chinese gudgeon, *Bostrichthys sinensis* (Lacepede), 10 cm TL, from one meter depth, West Lewis Island, Dampier Archipelago.

473. Whiskered goby, *Callogobius* species, 6 cm TL, from 2 meters depth, Houtman Abrolhos.

474. Sculptured goby, *Callogobius mucosus* (Guenther), 6 cm TL, from one meter depth, Geographe Bay.

475. Dusky finned goby, *Callogobius snelliusi* Koumans, about 5 cm TL, in 3 meters depth, Lady Nora Island, Dampier Archipelago.

476. Silhouette goby, *Silhouettea insinuans* Smith, 4 cm TL, from one meter depth, North West Cape.

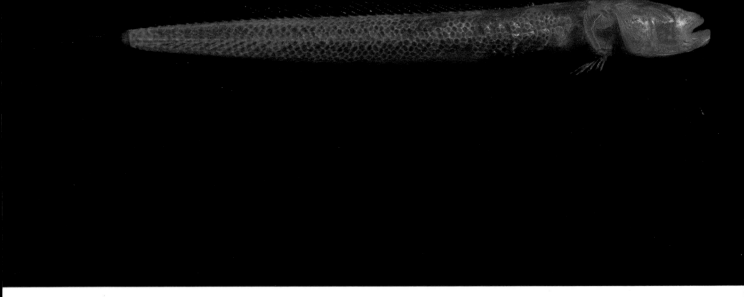

477. Blind goby, *Brachyamblyopus coecus* (Weber), 7 cm TL, from one meter depth, Prince Regent River.

478. Moorish idol, *Zanclus cornutus* (Linnaeus), about 22 cm TL, in 10 meters depth, Christmas Island, Indian Ocean.

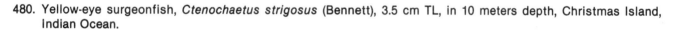

479. Clown surgeonfish, *Naso lituratus* (Bloch & Schneider), about 16 cm TL, in 6 meters depth, Kendrew Island, Dampier Archipelago.

480. Yellow-eye surgeonfish, *Ctenochaetus strigosus* (Bennett), 3.5 cm TL, in 10 meters depth, Christmas Island, Indian Ocean.

481. Whitespotted rabbitfish, *Siganus canaliculatus* (Park), 4 cm TL, from 3 meters depth, Rosemary Island, Dampier Archipelago.

482. Fuscous rabbitfish, *Siganus fuscescens* Houttuyn, about 25 cm TL, in 10 meters depth, Houtman Abrolhos.

483. Two barred rabbitfish, *Siganus doliatus* (Valenciennes), about 25 cm TL, in 12 meters depth, North West Cape.

484. Three-spot rabbitfish, *Siganus trispilos* Woodland & Allen, 22 cm TL, from 4 meters depth, North West Cape.

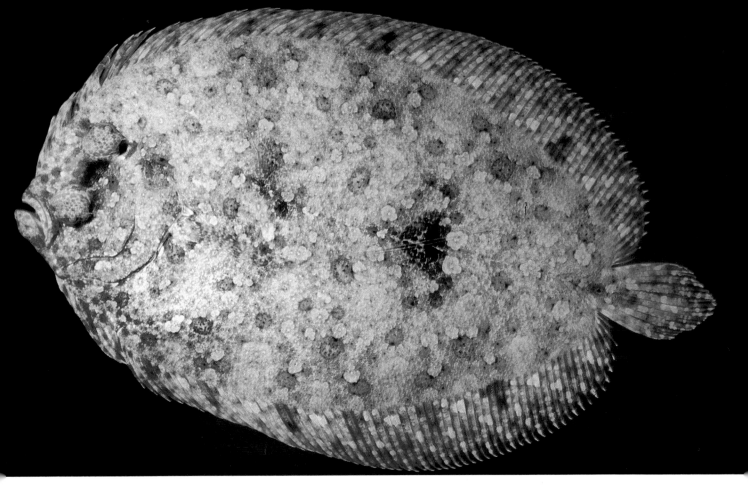

485. Panther flounder, *Bothus pantherinus* (Rueppell), 18 cm TL, from 2 meters depth, Houtman Abrolhos.

486. Jenyn's flounder, *Pseudorhombus jenynsii* (Bleeker), 12 cm TL, from 10 meters depth, Cockburn Sound.

487. Aesop sole, *Aesopia heterorhinos* (Bleeker), 8 cm TL, from 5 meters depth, Kendrew Island, Dampier Archipelago. Photo by B. Wilson.

488. Golden finned triggerfish, *Sufflamen chrysopterus* (Bloch & Schneider), about 22 cm TL, in 12 meters depth, North West Cape.

489. Reef triggerfish, *Sufflamen bursa* (Bloch & Schneider), about 22 cm TL, in 2 meters depth, Christmas Island, Indian Ocean.

490. Blue-lined triggerfish, *Pseudobalistes fuscus* (Bloch & Schneider), about 24 cm TL, in 13 meters depth, North West Cape.

491. Blue-lined triggerfish, *Pseudobalistes fuscus* (Bloch & Schneider), 5 cm TL, from 5 meters depth, Kendrew Island, Dampier Archipelago.

492. Bridled leatherjacket, *Acanthaluteres spilomelanurus* (Quoy & Gaimard), 8 cm TL, from 4 meters depth, Cockburn Sound.

493. Toothbrush leatherjacket, *Penicipelta vittiger* (Castelnau), 8 cm TL, from 10 meters depth, Rottnest Island.

494. Toothbrush leatherjacket, *Penicipelta vittiger* (Castelnau), about 10 cm TL, in 8 meters depth, Geographe Bay.

495. Rough leatherjacket, *Scobinichthys granulatus* (Shaw), 7 cm TL, from 10 meters depth, Cockburn Sound.

496. Rough leatherjacket, *Scobinichthys granulatus* (Shaw), about 10 cm TL, in 10 meters depth, Geographe Bay.

497. Blue-lined leatherjacket, *Meuschenia galii* (Waite), about 23 cm TL, in 10 meters depth, Recherche Archipelago.

498. Yellow-striped leatherjacket, *Meuschenia flavolineata* Hutchins, about 20 cm TL, in 5 meters depth, Geographe Bay.

499. Pygmy leatherjacket, *Brachaluteres jacksonianus* (Quoy & Gaimard), 4 cm TL, from 3 meters depth, Cockburn Sound.

500. Pygmy leatherjacket, *Brachaluteres jacksonianus* (Quoy & Gaimard), 3 cm TL, from 3 meters depth, Cockburn Sound.

501. Yellow-striped leatherjacket, *Meuschenia flavolineata* Hutchins, about 18 cm TL, in 5 meters depth, Recherche Archipelago.

502. Stars and stripes leatherjacket, *Meuschenia venusta* Hutchins, about 18 cm TL, in 6 meters depth, Recherche Archipelago.

503. Horseshoe leatherjacket, *Meuschenia hippocrepis* (Quoy and Gaimard), about 24 cm TL, at 4 meters depth, Garden Island.

504. Mosaic leatherjacket, *Eubalichthys mosaicus* (Ramsay & Ogilby), 30 cm TL, from 10 meters depth, Carnac Island.

505. Fan-bellied leatherjacket, *Monacanthus chinensis* Osbeck, 5 cm TL, from 4 meters depth, Cockburn Sound.

506. Fan-bellied leatherjacket, *Monacanthus chinensis* Osbeck, 13 cm TL, from 6 meters depth, Houtman Abrolhos.

507. Redtail leatherjacket, *Pervagor janthinosoma* (Bleeker), 12 cm TL, from 10 meters depth, North West Cape.

508. Indo-Pacific leatherjacket, *Cantherhines pardalis* (Rueppell), about 14 cm TL, in 12 meters depth, North West Cape.

509. White-barred boxfish, *Anoplocapros lenticularis* (Richardson), about 5 cm TL, in 5 meters depth, Garden Island.

510. White-barred boxfish, *Anoplocapros lenticularis* (Richardson), about 12 cm TL, in 18 meters depth, Rottnest Island.

511. Shaw's cowfish, *Aracana aurita* (Shaw & Nodder), about 16 cm TL, in 5 meters depth, Rottnest Island.

512. Shaw's cowfish, *Aracana aurita* (Shaw & Nodder), about 10 cm TL, in 6 meters depth, Geographe Bay.

513. Golden boxfish, *Strophiurichthys robustus* Fraser-Brunner, 13 cm TL, from 5 meters depth, Houtman Abrolhos.

514. Cowfish, *Lactoria cornuta* (Linnaeus), about 10 cm TL, in 5 meters depth, Kendrew Island, Dampier Archipelago.

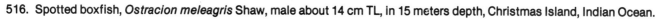

515. Polka dot boxfish, *Ostracion cubicus* Linnaeus, about 10 cm TL, in 3 meters depth, Rosemary Island, Dampier Archipelago.

516. Spotted boxfish, *Ostracion meleagris* Shaw, male about 14 cm TL, in 15 meters depth, Christmas Island, Indian Ocean.

517. Broad barred puffer, *Arothron hispidus* (Linneaus), about 20 cm TL, in 3 meters depth, North West Cape.

518. Narrow lined puffer, *Arothron immaculatus* (Bloch & Schneider), about 18 cm TL, in 2 meters depth, Lady Nora Island, Dampier Archipelago.

519. Starry puffer, *Arothron stellatus* (Bloch & Schneider), 15 cm TL, from 4 meters depth, North West Cape.

520. Black spotted pufferfish (yellow phase), *Arothron nigropunctatus* (Bloch & Schneider), about 40 cm TL, in 30 meters depth, Christmas Island, Indian Ocean.

521. Sharpnosed puffer, *Canthigaster coronatus* (Vaillant & Sauvage), 8 cm TL, from 15 meters depth, North West Cape.

522. Ringed puffer, *Omegophora armilla* (McCulloch & Waite), about 14 cm TL, in 10 meters depth, Geographe Bay.

523. Blue-spotted puffer, *Omegophora cyanopunctata* Hardy & Hutchins, about 12 cm TL, in 8 meters depth, Geographe Bay.

524. Common blowfish, *Torquigener pleurogramma* (Regan), 5 cm TL, from one meter depth, Houtman Abrolhos.

525. Southern porcupinefish, *Diodon nicthemerus* Cuvier, 5 cm TL, from 2 meters depth, Cockburn Sound.

526. Fixed spine porcupinefish, *Chilomycterus orbicularis* (Bloch), about 18 cm TL, in 3 meters depth, Kendrew Island, Dampier Archipelago.

APPENDIX
PROVISIONAL CHECKLIST OF THE MARINE FISHES OF WESTERN AUSTRALIA

Note: This list includes fishes collected off Western Australia to July 1984. Species that have their main distribution below 100 meters depth and those generally considered as deepsea and midwater oceanic dwellers are mostly excluded. Family names are given in all capital letters. Species marked with a star are cool water fishes generally found south of 28°S latitude or roughly the Houtman Abrolhos (species without this symbol are chiefly tropical or subtropical in distribution). Endemic fishes are enclosed in brackets. Most of the species listed are represented by preserved specimens deposited at the Western Australian Museum, Perth.

GEOTRIIDAE

Geotria australis Gray

HETERODONTIDAE

Heterodontus portusjacksoni Meyer

ODONTASPIDIDAE

Odontaspis taurus (Rafinesque)

LAMNIDAE

Carcharodon carcharias (Linnaeus)
Isurus oxyrinchus Rafinesque
Lamna whitleyi Phillipps

CETORHINIDAE

Cetorhinus maximus (Gunnerus)

HEXANCHIDAE

Heptranchias perlo (Bonnaterre)

ALOPIIDAE

Alopias caudatus Phillipps

ORECTOLOBIDAE

Brachaelurus waddi (Bloch & Schneider)
Chiloscyllium punctatum Müller & Henle
Eucrossorhinus ogilbyi (Regan)
Ginglymostoma ferrugineum (Lesson)
Hemiscyllium ocellatum (Bonnaterre)

H. trispeculare Richardson
Orectolobus halei Whitley
O. maculatus (Bonnaterre)
O. tentaculatus (Peters)
O. wardi Whitley
[O. sp.]
Parascyllium ferrugineum McCulloch
P. variolatum Dumeril
Stegostoma tigrinum (Pennant)

RHINCODONTIDAE

Rhincodon typus Smith

SCYLIORHINIDAE

Asymbolus analis (Ogilby)
Atelomycterus marmoratum (Bennett)
[*Aulohalaelurus labiosus* (Waite)]
Cephaloscyllium laticeps (Dumeril)
Galeus boardmani (Whitley)
Halaelurus boesemani Springer & D'Aubrey
Juncrus vincenti (Zietz)

TRIAKIDAE
Furgaleus ventralis (Whitley)
Mustelus antarcticus Günther

CARCHARHINIDAE

Carcharhinus altimus (Springer)
C. amblyrhynchos (Bleeker)
C. amboinensis (Müller & Henle)
C. brachyurus (Günther)
C. brevipinna (Müller & Henle)
C. cautus Whitley
C. leucas (Müller & Henle)

C. limbatus (Müller & Henle)
C. longimanus (Poey)
C. melanopterus (Quoy & Gaimard)
C. obscurus Le Sueur
C. plumbeus (Nardo)
C. sealei (Pietschmann)
C. sorrah (Müller & Henle)
Galeocerdo cuvieri (Le Sueur)
Galeorhinus australis (Macleay)
Hemipristis elongatus (Klunzinger)
Loxodon macrorhinus Müller & Henle)
Negaprion acutidens (Rüppell)
Neogaleus microstoma (Bleeker)
Prionace glauca (Linnaeus)
Rhizoprionodon acutus (Rüppell)
R. taylori (Ogilby)
Triaenodon obesus (Rüppell)

SPHYRNIDAE

Sphyrna lewini (Griffith)
S. zygaena (Linnaeus)

OXYNOTIDAE

Oxynotus bruniensis (Ogilby)

SQUALIDAE

Deania quadrispinosa (McCulloch)
Etmopterus lucifer Jordan & Snyder
Squalus acanthias Linnaeus
S. blainvillei (Risso)
S. megalops (Macleay)

DALATIIDAE

Dalatias licha (Bonnaterre)

Euprotomicrus bispinatus (Quoy &
   Gaimard)
Isistius brasiliensis (Quoy & Gaimard)

ECHINORHINIDAE

Echinorhinus brucus (Bonnaterre)

PRISTIOPHORIDAE

Pristiophorus cirratus (Latham)
P. nudipinnis Günther

SQUATINIDAE

Squatina australis Regan
S. tergocellata McCulloch

PRISTIDAE

Pristiopsis leichardti Whitley
Pristis clavata Garman
P. zijsron Bleeker

RHYNCHOBATIDAE

Rhynchobatus djiddensis (Forsskal)

RHINOBATIDAE

Aptychotremata vincentiana (Haacke)
Rhinobatus armatus (Gray)
R. dumerilii Castelnau
Trygonorhina fasciata Müller &
   Henle

TORPEDINIDAE

Hypnos monopterygium (Shaw &
   Nodder)
[*Narcine westraliensis* McKay]
Torpedo macneilii (Whitley)

RAJIDAE

[*Pavoraja alleni* McEachran &
   Fechhelm]
Psammobatus waitii (McCulloch)
Raja gudgeri Whitley

DASYATIDIDAE

Amphotistius kuhlii (Müller & Henle)
Dasyatis brevicaudata (Hutton)
D. sephen (Forsskal)
D. thetidis Waite

Himantura uarnak Forsskal
Taeniura lymma (Forsskal)
Urogymnus asperrimus (Bloch &
   Schneider)

GYMNURIDAE

Gymnura australis (Ramsay &
   Ogilby)

UROLOPHIDAE

[*Urolophus circularis* McKay]
U. gigas (Scott)
[*U. lobatus* McKay]
U. mucosus Whitley
U. paucimaculatus (Scott)
U. spp. (6)

MYLIOBATIDAE

Aetobatus narinari (Euphrasen)
Myliobatis australis Macleay

RHINOPTERIDAE

Rhinoptera neglecta Ogilby

MOBULIDAE

Manta birostris (Walbaum)

CHIMAERIDAE

Hydrolagus ogilbyi (Waite)

ELOPIDAE

Elops hawaiiensis Regan

MEGALOPIDAE

Megalops cyprinoides (Broussonet)

ANGUILLIDAE

Anguilla bicolor McClelland

MURAENIDAE

Anarchias fuscus Smith
Echidna nebulosa (Ahl)
E. polyzona (Richardson)
E. unicolor Schultz
E. zebra (Shaw)
Gymnothorax buroensis (Bleeker)

G. eurostus (Abbott)
G. favagineus Bloch & Schneider
G. flavimarginatus (Rüppell)
G. fuscomaculatus (Schultz)
G. javanicus (Bleeker)
G. margaritophora (Bleeker)
G. melanospilus (Bleeker)
G. melatremus Schultz
G. monochrous Bleeker
G. pictus (Ahl)
G. prasinus (Richardson)
G. thrysoideus (Richardson)
G. undulatus (Lacépède)
[*G. woodwardi* McCulloch]
G. zonipectus Seale
G. sp.
Uropterygius concolor Rüppell

MURAENESOCIDAE

Muraenesox cinereus (Forsskal)

CONGRIDAE

Conger cinereus Rüppell
C. wilsoni (Bloch & Schneider)
Gnathophis habenatus (Richardson)

OPHICHTHIDAE

Brachysomophis cirrhocheilos (Bleeker)
Callechelys marmoratus (Bleeker)
Cirrhimuraena calamus (Günther)
Leiuranus semicinctus (Lay &
   Bennett)
Muraenichthys australis Macleay
M. breviceps Günther
M. gymnotus (Bleeker)
M. macropterus (Bleeker)
M. ogilbyi Fowler
M. tasmaniensis McCulloch
Myrichthys colubrinus (Boddaert)
Myrophis sp.
Ophichthus celebicus (Bleeker)
O. cephalozona (Bleeker)
O. rutidodermatoides (Bleeker)
O. melanochir Bleeker
Ophisurus serpens (Linnaeus)
Phyllophichthus xenodontus Gosline
Pisodonophis boro (Hamilton)
P. cancrivorus (Richardson)
Yirrkala lumbricoides (Bleeker)

CLUPEIDAE

Amblygaster leiogaster (Valenciennes)

A. sirm (Walbaum)
Anodontostoma chacunda (Hamilton)
Dussumieria acuta (Valenciennes)
Escualosa thoracata (Valenciennes)
*Etrumeus teres (DeKay)
Herklotsichthys blackburni (Whitley)
H. koningsbergeri (Weber & De Beaufort)
H. lippa (Whitley)
H. maccullochi (Whitley)
H. quadrimaculatus (Rüppell)
*Hyperlophus vittatus (Castelnau)
Ilisha striatula Thosaporn
Nematalosa come (Richardson)
*N. vlaminghi (Munro)
Pellona ditchela Valenciennes
Sardinella albella (Valenciennes)
S. brachysoma Bleeker
S. gibbosa (Bleeker)
S. lemuru Bleeker
*Sardinops neopilchardus (Steindachner)
Spratelloides gracilis (Schlegel)
S. robustus Ogilby

ENGRAULIDAE

*Engraulis australis (Shaw)
Setipinna papuensis Munro
S. tenuifilis (Valenciennes)
Stolephorus buccaneeri Strasburg
S. heterolobus (Rüppell)
S. indicus (Van Hasselt)
Thrissina baelama (Forsskal)
Thryssa hamiltoni (Gray)
T. scratchleyi (Ramsay & Ogilby)
T. setirostris (Broussonet)

CHIROCENTRIDAE

Chirocentrus dorab (Forsskal)

AULOPIDAE

*Aulopus purpurissatus Richardson

SYNODONTIDAE

Saurida gracilis (Quoy & Gaimard)
S. tumbil (Bloch)
S. undosquamis (Richardson)
Synodus jaculum Russell & Cressey
S. sageneus Waite
S. similis McCulloch
S. variegatus (Lacépède)
Trachinocephalus myops (Schneider)

GONORHYNCHIDAE

*Gonorhynchus greyi (Richardson)

CHANIDAE

Chanos chanos (Forsskal)

ARIIDAE

Arius armiger De Vis
A. graeffei Kner & Steindachner
A. mastersi Ogilby
A. proximus Ogilby
A. thalassina (Rüppell)

PLOTOSIDAE

*Cnidoglanis macrocephalus (Valenciennes)
C. microceps (Richardson)
Euristhmus lepturus (Günther)
E. nudiceps (Günther)
Paraplotosus albilabrus (Valenciennes)
[*P.* sp.]
Plotosus canius Hamilton
P. lineatus (Thunberg)

BATRACHOIDIDAE

Batrachomoeus dahli (Rendahl)
[*B. occidentalis* Hutchins]
[**B. rubricephalus* Hutchins]
B. trispinosus (Günther)
Halophryne diemensis (Le Sueur)
H. ocellatus Hutchins

GOBIESOCIDAE

*Alabes brevis Springer & Fraser
*A. dorsalis (Richardson)
*A. parvulus (McCulloch)
*Aspasmogaster liorhynchus Briggs
[**A. occidentalis* Hutchins]
*A. tasmaniensis (Günther)
*Cochleoceps spatula (Günther)
Diademichthys lineatus (Sauvage)
[*Lepadichthys sandaracatus* Whitley]
*Parviceps parvipinnis (Waite)
**gobiesocid spp. (10)

ANTENNARIIDAE

[**Allenichthys glauerti* (Whitley)]
Antennarius analis (Gosline)
A. coccineus (Cuvier)

A. dorehensis Bleeker
A. hispidus (Bloch & Schneider)
A. nummifer (Cuvier)
A. striatus (Shaw & Nodder)
*Echinophryne crassispina (McCulloch & Waite)
*E. sp.
Histiophryne bougainvilli (Valenciennes)
H. cryptacanthus (Weber)
Histrio histrio (Linnaeus)
*Kuiterichthys sp.
Lophiocharon trisignatus (Richardson)
*Phyllophryne scortea (McCulloch & Waite)
*Rhycherus gloveri Pietsch
Tathicarpus butleri Ogilby

TETRABRACHIIDAE

Tetrabrachium ocellatum Günther

CHAUNACIDAE

Lophiomus laticeps (Ogilby)

MORIDAE

*Lotella fuliginosa Günther
*L. rhacinus (Forster)
*Pseudophycis barbatus (Günther)
*P. breviusculus Richardson

BYTHITIDAE

Brosomophyciops sp.
*Dermatopsis multiradiata McCulloch & Waite
[**Dinematichthys dasyrhynchus* Cohen & Hutchins]
Dipulus caecus Waite
*Monothrix polylepis (Ogilby)
Ogilbia spp. (3)

OPHIDIIDAE

Brotula multibarbata Temminck & Schlegel
*Dannevigia tusca Whitley
*Genypterus blacodes (Bloch & Schneider)
Ophidion muraenolepis (Günther)

CARAPIDAE

Carapus margaritiferae (Rendahl)

EXOCOETIDAE

Cypselurus altipennis (Valenciennes)
C. arcticeps (Günther)
C. furcatus (Mitchill)
C. nigripennis (Valenciennes)
Hirundichthys speculiger
  (Valenciennes)
Oxyporhamphus argenteus (Bennett)
Parexocoetus brachypterus
  (Richardson)

HEMIRAMPHIDAE

Arrhamphus sclerolepis Günther
Euleptorhamphus viridis (van Hasselt)
Hemiramphus far (Forsskal)
H. robustus Günther
Hyporhamphus affinis (Günther)
H. dussumieri (Valenciennes)
*H. melanochir (Valenciennes)
H. neglectus (Bleeker)
H. quoyi (Valenciennes)
*H. regularis regularis (Günther)
Zenarchopterus buffonis
  (Valenciennes)

BELONIDAE

Ablennes hians (Valenciennes)
Platybelone argalus (Le Sueur)
Strongylura leiura (Bleeker)
S. strongylura (van Hasselt)
Tylosurus crocodilus (Peron &
  Le Sueur)
T. gavialoides (Castelnau)

SCOMBERESOCIDAE

*Scomberesox saurus (Bloch &.
  Schneider)

ATHERINIDAE

Allanetta mugiloides (McCulloch)
*Atherinosoma elongata (Klunzinger)
A. presbyteroides (Richardson)
[**A. wallacei* Prince, Ivantsoff, &
  Potter]
[*Craterocephalus pauciradiatus*
  (Günther)]
Hypoatherina temminckii (Bleeker)
Pranesus endrachtensis (Quoy &
  Gaimard)
P. ogilbyi Whitley

ISONIDAE

*Iso rhothophilus (Ogilby)

TRACHICHTHYIDAE

[**Optivus* sp.]
*Paratrachichthys trailli (Hutton)
Sorosichthys ananassa Whitley
*Trachichthys australis Shaw &
  Nodder

BERYCIDAE

*Centroberyx gerrardi (Günther)
*C. lineatus (Cuvier)
C. sp.

MONOCENTRIDAE

Cleidopus gloriamaris De Vis
Monocentrus japonicus (Houttuyn)

HOLOCENTRIDAE

Myripristis adustus Bleeker
M. hexagonatus (Lacépède)
M. kuntee Cuvier
M. melanostictus Bleeker
M. murdjan (Forsskal)
Neoniphon sammara (Forsskal)
Ostichthys kaianus Günther
Pristilepis oligolepis (Whitley)
Sargocentron diadema (Lacépède)
S. lepros (Allen & Cross)
S. punctatissimum (Cuvier)
S. ruber (Forsskal)
S. spinifer (Forsskal)
S. tiere (Cuvier)
S. violaceus (Bleeker)

MACRUROCYTTIDAE

Cyttus hololepis Goode & Bean

ZEIDAE

*Zenopsis australis (Richardson)
Z. nebulosa (Temminck & Schlegel)
*Zeus faber Linnaeus

VELIFERIDAE

Velifer hypselopterus Bleeker
V. multiradiatus Regan

AULOSTOMIDAE

Aulostomus chinensis (Linnaeus)

FISTULARIIDAE

Fistularia commersonii Rüppell
F. petimba Lacépède

REGALECIDAE

*Regalecus glesne Ascanius

MACRORHAMPHOSIDAE

*Centriscops humerosus (Richardson)
*Macrorhamphosus elevatus Waite
*Notopogon lilliei Regan

CENTRISCIDAE

Centriscus cristatus (De Vis)
C. scutatus (Linnaeus)

SOLENOSTOMIDAE

Solenichthys cyanopterus (Bleeker)
Solenostomus paradoxus (Pallas)

SYNGNATHIDAE

*Acentronura australe Waite & Hale
  [*A. larsonae* Dawson]
Bulbonaricus brauni (Dawson &
  Allen)
*Campichthys galei (Duncker)
C. tricarinatus Dawson
Choeroichthys brachysoma (Bleeker)
[*C. latispinosus* Dawson]
C. suillus Whitley
Doryrhamphus janssi (Herald &
  Randall)
[*Festucalex scalaris* (Günther)]
Filicampus tigris (Castelnau)
Halicampus brocki (Schultz)
H. grayi Kaup
H. spinirostris (Dawson & Allen)
Haliichthys taeniophorus Gray
*Heraldia nocturna Paxton
Hippichthys penicillus (Cantor)
*Hippocampus angustus Günther
*H. breviceps Peters
[*H. planifrons* Peters]
H. spinosissimus Weber
*Histiogamphelus cristatus (Macleay)
*Leptoichthys fistularius Kaup
*Lissocampus caudalis Waite & Hale
L. fatiloquus (Whitley)
*L. runa (Whitley)
*Maroubra perserrata Whitley

Micrognathus micronotopterus (Fowler)
[*Mitotichthys meraculus* (Whitley)]
Nannocampus subosseus Günther
Notiocampus ruber (Ramsay &
Ogilby)
Parasyngnathus argyrostictus (Kaup)
Phyllopteryx taeniolatus Lacépède
Phycodurus eques Günther)
Pugnaso curtirostris Castelnau)
Solegnathus hardwickii (Gray)
S. lettiensis Bleeker
Stigmatopora argus (Richardson)
S. nigra Kaup
Syngnathoides biaculeatus (Bloch)
Trachyrhamphus bicoarctata (Bleeker)
T. longirostris Kaup
Urocampus carinirostris Castelnau
Vanacampus margaritifer (Peters)
V. phillipi (Lucas)
V. poecilolaemus (Peters)

SCORPAENIDAE

Ablabys taenianotus (Cuvier)
Apistops caloundra (De Vis)
Centropogon latifrons Mees
Cheroscorpaena tridactyla Mees
Cottapistus cottoides Cuvier
Dampierosa daruma Whitley
Dendochirus brachypterus (Cuvier)
D. zebra (Quoy & Gaimard)
Erosa erosa (Langsdorf)
Glyptauchen panduratus (Richardson)
Gymnapistes marmoratus (Cuvier)
Helicolenus papillosus (Bloch &
Schneider)
Hypodytes carinatus (Bloch &
Schneider)
Inimicus didactylus (Pallas)
I. sinensis (Valenciennes)
Liocranium praepositum Ogilby
L. scorpio (Ogilby)
[*Maxillicosta lopholepis* Eschmeyer &
Poss]
M. scabriceps Whitley
Minous monodactylus (Bloch &
Schneider)
Neosebastes nigropunctatus
McCulloch
N. pandus (Richardson)
N. panticus McCulloch & Waite
N. thetidis (Waite)
Paracentropogon vespa Ogilby
Peristrominous dolosus Whitley
Pteroidichthys godfreyi (Whitley)
Pterois antennata (Bloch)

P. russelli Bennett
P. volitans (Linnaeus)
Richardsonichthys leucogaster
(Richardson)
Scorpaena ergastulorum Richardson
S. oglinus (Smith)
S. picta Cuvier
[*S. sumptuosa* Castelnau]
S. sp.
Scorpaenodes guamensis (Quoy &
Gaimard)
S. littoralis (Tanaka)
[*S. steenei* Allen]
S. varipinnis Smith
S. sp.
Scorpaenopsis cirrhosa (Thunberg)
S. diabolus (Cuvier)
Setarches guentheri Johnson
S. longiceps Günther
Synanceia gibbosa (Bloch &
Schneider)
S. horrida (Linnaeus)

APLOACTINIDAE

Acanthosophex sp.
Adventor elongatus (Whitley)
Aploactis aspersa Temminck &
Schlegel
Aploactisoma milesii (Richardson)
Bathyaploactis curtisensis Whitley
Cocotropus sp.
Kanekonia queenslandica Whitley
Karumba ornatissima (Whitley)
Neoaploactis tridorsalis Eschmeyer &
Allen
[*Paraploactis intonsa* Poss &
Eschmeyer]
[*P. pulvinus* Poss & Eschmeyer]

TRIGLIDAE

Chelidonichthys kumu (Lesson &
Garnot)
Lepidotrigla modesta Waite
Paratrigla papilio (Cuvier)
Peristedion sp.
Pterygotrigla polyommata
(Richardson)

PATAECIDAE

Aetapcus maculatus Günther
Gnathanacanthus goetzeei Bleeker
Neopataecus waterhousii (Castelnau)
Pataecus fronto Richardson

PLATYCEPHALIDAE

Elates ransonneti (Steindachner)
Insidiator diversidens McCulloch
Platycephalus cirronasus Richardson
P. endractensis Quoy & Gaimard
P. fuscus Cuvier
P. harrisi McCulloch
P. inops (Jenyns)
P. isacanthus Cuvier
P. laevigata Cuvier
P. longispinus Macleay
P. malayanus Bleeker
P. nematophthalmus Günther
P. oligolepis Regan
P. rodericensis Cuvier
P. speculator Klunzinger
P. spinosus Temminck & Schlegel
P. tuberculatus Cuvier

HOPLICHTHYIDAE

Hoplichthys ogilbyi McCulloch

CONGIOPODIDAE

Congiopodus leucometopon (Waite)
C. leucopaecilus (Richardson)

DACTYLOPTERIDAE

Dactyloptaena orientalis (Cuvier)

PEGASIDAE

Parapegasus natans (Linnaeus)

AMBASSIDAE

Ambassis interrupta Bleeker
A. nalua (Hamilton)
A. vachelli Richardson

CENTROPOMIDAE

Hypopterus macropterus (Günther)
Lates calcarifer (Bloch)
Psammoperca waigiensis (Cuvier)

SERRANIDAE

[*Acanthistius pardalotus* Hutchins]
[*A. serratus* (Cuvier)]
Anyperodon leucogrammicus
(Valenciennes)

Centrogenys vaigiensis Quoy &
  Gaimard
Cephalopholis argus Bloch
C. boenack (Bloch)
C. formosa (Shaw)
C. leopardus (Lacépède)
C. miniata (Forsskal)
C. rogaa (Forsskal)
C. sonnerati (Valenciennes)
C. urodelus (Valenciennes)
C. sp.
Cromileptes altivelis (Valenciennes)
Epinephelus amblycephalus (Bleeker)
E. areolatus (Forsskal)
E. caeruleopunctatus (Bloch)
E. chlorostigma (Valenciennces)
E. corallicola (Valenciennes)
E. fasciatus (Forsskal)
E. fuscoguttatus (Forsskal)
E. latifasciatus (Temminck &
  Schlegel)
E. maculatus (Bloch)
E. merra Bloch
E. microdon (Bleeker)
E. multinotatus (Peters)
E. quoyanus (Valenciennes)
E. rivulatus (Valenciennes)
★E. septemfasciatus (Thunberg)
E. sexfasciatus (Valenciennes)
E. suillus (Valenciennes)
E. tukula Morgans
E. woorei (Whitley)
Plectropomus leopardus (Lacépéde)
P. maculatus (Bloch)
P. truncatus Fowler & Bean
★Polyprion americanus (Bloch &
  Schneider)
★P. oxygeneois (Bloch & Schneider)
Promicrops lanceolatus (Bloch)
Variola louti (Forsskal)

SERRANIDAE [subfamily
ANTHIINAE]

[*Anthias georgei* Allen]
A. kashiwae (Tanaka)
A. pulchellus Waite
A. rubrizonatus Randall
★Caesioperca lepidoptera (Bloch &
  Schneider)
★C. rasor (Richardson)
[*★C.* sp.]
[*★Callanthias allporti* Günther]
Caprodon schlegeli (Günther)
[*★Ellerkeldia rubra* Allen]
[*★E. wilsoni* Allen & Moyer]

[*★Epinephelides armatus* (Castelnau)]
★Hypoplectrodes nigrorubrum (Cuvier)
[*★Lepidoperca occidentalis* Whitley]
★Othos dentex (Cuvier)
[*★Plectranthias alleni* Randall]
P. japonicus (Steindachner)
P. megalophthalmus Fourmanoir &
  Randall
P. wheeleri Randall
[*Sacura parva* Heemstra & Randall]
Selenanthias analis Tanaka

GRAMMISTIDAE

Diploprion bifasciatum Cuvier
Grammistes sexlineatus (Thunberg)
Rainfordia opercularis McCulloch

PSEUDOCHROMIDAE

Labracinus lineatus (Castelnau)
Pseudochromis bitaeniatus (Fowler)
P. fuscus Müller & Troschel
P. marshallensis Schultz
P. punctatus (Richardson)
P. quinquedentatus McCulloch
P. tapeinosoma Bleeker
P. wilsoni Whitley
Pseudoplesiops rosae Schultz

PSEUDOGRAMMIDAE

Pseudogramma polyacantha (Bleeker)

PLESIOPIDAE

Calloplesiops altivelis (Steindachner)
★Paraplesiops meleagris Peters
★P. sp.
Plesiops coeruleolineatus Rüppell
★Trachinops brauni Allen
T. noarlungae Glover

ACANTHOCLINIDAE

★Acanthoplesiops sp.
Belonepterygium fasciolatum (Ogilby)

GLAUCOSOMATIDAE

Glaucosoma buergeri Richardson
[*★G. hebraicum* Richardson]
G. magnifica Ogilby

TERAPONIDAE

Amniataba caudavittatus (Richardson)
★Helotes sexlineatus Quoy & Gaimard
Pelates quadrilineatus (Bloch)
★Pelsartia humeralis Ogilby
Terapon jarbua (Forsskal)
T. puta Cuvier
T. theraps Cuvier

BANJOSIDAE

Banjos banjos (Richardson)

PRIACANTHIDAE

Cookeolus boops (Schneider)
Priacanthus cruentatus (Lacépède)
P. hamrur (Forsskal)
P. macracanthus Cuvier
P. tayenus Richardson
Pristigenys niphonia (Cuvier)

APOGONIDAE

Apogon angustatus (Smith &
  Radcliffe)
A. aureus (Lacépède)
A. bandanensis Bleeker
A. brevicaudatus Weber
A. carinatus Cuvier
A. chrysotaenia Bleeker
A. coccineus Rüppell
A. cooki Macleay
A. crassiceps Garman
A. cyanosoma (Bleeker)
A. darnleyensis Alleyne & Macleay
A. doederleini Jordan & Snyder
A. ellioti Day
A. endekataenia (Bleeker)
A. evermanni Jordan & Snyder
A. fasciatus (White)
A. fraenatus Valenciennes
A. hartzfeldi Bleeker
A. kallopterus Bleeker
A. moluccensis Valenciennes
A. nigripinnis Cuvier
A. poecilopterus Cuvier
A. quadrifasciatus Cuvier
A. ruppelli Günther
A. savayensis Günther
A. semilineatus Temminck & Schlegel
A. semiornatus Peters
A. septemstriatus Günther
A. taeniophorus Regan
A. trimaculatus Cuvier
[*★A. victoriae* (Günther)]
A. sp.

Archamia fucata (Cantor)
A. melasma Lachner & Taylor
Cheilodipterus lachneri Klausewitz
C. lineatus Lacépède
C. quinquelineata Cuvier
Foa fo Jordan & Seale
Fowleria aurita (Valenciennes)
F. variegata (Valenciennes)
[*Pterapogon mirifica* (Mees)]
Rhabdamia cypselurus Weber
R. gracilis (Bleeker)
R. sp.
Siphamia argyrogaster Weber
★S. cephalotes (Castelnau)
S. cuneiceps Whitley
S. majimae Matsubara & Iwai
★*Vincentia punctatus* (Klunzinger)
★*V.* spp. (2)

DINOLESTIDAE

★*Dinolestes lewini* (Griffith)

SILLAGINIDAE

Sillago analis Whitley
★*S. bassensis* Cuvier
S. maculata Quoy & Gaimard
S. robusta Stead
★*S. schombergki* Peters
S. spp. (2)
★*Sillaginoides punctata* Cuvier

POMATOMIDAE

Pomatomus saltatrix (Linnaeus)

RACHYCENTRIDAE

Rachycentron canadum (Linnaeus)

ECHENEIDAE

Echeneis australis Bennett
E. naucrates Linnaeus
E. osteochir Cuvier
E. remora Linnaeus

CARANGIDAE

Alectis ciliaris (Bloch)
Alectis indicus (Rüppell)
Alepes n. sp.
Atule mate (Cuvier)
Carangoides bajad (Forsskal)
C. caeruleopinnatus (Rüppell)
C. chrysophrys (Cuvier)

C. equula (Temminck and Schlegel)
C. ferdau (Forsskal)
C. fulvoguttatus (Forsskal)
C. gymnostethus (Cuvier)
C. humerosus (McCulloch)
C. malabaricus (Bloch and Schneider)
C. orthogrammus Jordan and Gilbert
C. talamparoides Bleeker
C. sp.
Caranx bucculentus Alleyne and Macleay
C. ignobilis (Forsskal)
C. lugubris Poey
C. melampygus Cuvier
C. papuensis Alleyne and Macleay
C. sexfasciatus Quoy and Gaimard
Decapterus kurroides Bleeker
D. macarellus Cuvier
D. macrosoma Bleeker
D. russelli (Rüppell)
D. scombrinus (Valenciennes)
Elagatis bipinnulata (Quoy and Gaimard)
Gnathanodon speciosus (Forsskal)
Megalaspis cordyla (Linnaeus)
Naucrates ductor (Linnaeus)
Pantolabus radiatus (Macleay)
Parastromateus niger (Bloch)
Pseudocaranx dentex (Bloch and Schneider)
★*P. wrighti* (Whitley)
Scomberoides commersonnianus (Lacépède)
S. lysan (Forsskal)
S. tala (Cuvier)
S. tol (Cuvier)
Selar boops (Cuvier)
S. crumenophthalmus (Bloch)
Selaroides leptolepis (Cuvier)
Seriola hippos Günther
S. lalandi Valenciennes
Seriolina nigrofasciata (Rüppell)
Trachinotus baillonii (Lacépède)
T. blochii (Lacépède)
T. velox Ogilby
★*Trachurus declivis* (Jenyns)
★*T. novaezelandiae* Richardson
Ulua aurochs (Ogilby)
★*U. mentalis* Cuvier
Uraspis uraspis Günther

MENIDAE

Mene maculata (Bloch & Schneider)

LEIOGNATHIDAE

Gazza minuta (Bloch)
Leiognathus bindus (Valenciennes)
L. elongatus (Günther)
L. equulus (Forsskal)
L. hastatus Ogilby
L. leuciscus (Günther)
L. moretoniensis Ogilby
L. novaehollandiae (Steindachner)
L. nuchalis (Temminck & Schlegel)
L. smithhursti (Ramsay & Ogilby)
L. splendens (Cuvier)
L. sp.
Secutor ruconis (Hamilton)

ARRIPIDAE

★*Arripis georgianus* (Valenciennes)
★*A. esper* Whitley

EMMELICHTHYIDAE

★*Emmelichthys nitidus* Richardson
E. sp.
★*Plagiogeneion macrolepis* (McCulloch)

CAESIONIDAE

Caesio erythrogaster Cuvier
C. lunaris Cuvier
Pterocaesio diagramma (Bleeker)

CAESIOSCORPIDAE

[★*Caesioscorpis theagenes* Whitley]

LUTJANIDAE

Aphareus rutilans Cuvier
Aprion virescens Valenciennes
Etelis marshi (Jenkins)
Lipocheilus carnolabrum (Chan)
Lutjanus argentimaculatus (Forsskal)
L. bitaeniatus (Valenciennes)
L. bohar (Forsskal)
L. boutton (Lacépède)
L. carponotatus Richardson
L. decussatus (Cuvier)
L. erythropterus (Bloch)
L. fulviflammus (Forsskal)
L. kasmira (Forsskal)
L. lemniscatus (Valenciennes)
L. lutjanus Bloch
L. malabaricus (Schneider)
L. quinquelineatus (Bloch)
L. rivulatus (Cuvier)

L. russelli (Bleeker)
L. sebae (Cuvier)
L. vittus (Quoy & Gaimard)
Pristipomoides argyrogrammicus
  (Valenciennes)
P. microlepis (Bleeker)
Symphorus nematophorus (Bleeker)

NEMIPTERIDAE

Nemipterus bathybus Snyder
N. hexodon (Quoy & Gaimard)
N. metopias Bleeker
N. peronii (Valenciennes)
N. theodorei Ogilby
N. tolu (Valenciennes)
N. virgatus (Houttuyn)
Parascolopsis inermis (Temminck &
  Schlegel)
Pentapodus emeryii (Richardson)
P. nagasakiensis (Tanaka)
P. porosus (Valenciennes)
[*P. vitta* (Quoy & Gaimard)]
P. sp.
Scolopsis bilineatus (Bloch)
S. monogramma (Cuvier)
S. taeniopterus (Cuvier)
S. xenochrous Günther
[*Scaevius milii* (Bory)]

LOBOTIDAE

Lobotes surinamensis (Bloch)

GERREIDAE

Gerres filamentosus Cuvier
**G. subfasciatus* Cuvier
**Parequula melbournensis* (Castelnau)

HAEMULIDAE

Haplogenys kishinouyei Smith & Pope
Plectorhynchus chaetodonoides
  Lacépède
P. chubbi (Regan)
P. flavomaculatus (Cuvier)
P. multivittatus (Macleay)
P. nigrus (Cuvier)
P. pictus (Thunberg)
P. polytaenia (Bleeker)
P. sordidus (Klunzinger)
Pomadasys hasta (Bloch)
P. maculatum (Bloch)

LETHRINIDAE

Gnathodentex aureolineatus (Lacépède)
Gymnocranius elongatus Senta
G. griseus (Temminck & Schlegel)
G. robinsoni Gilchrist & Thompson
Lethrinella miniatus (Bloch &
  Schneider)
Lethrinus chrysostomus Richardson
L. laticaudus Alleyne & Macleay
L. nebulosus (Forsskal)
L. nematacanthus Bleeker
L. variegatus Valenciennes

SPARIDAE

**Acanthopagrus butcheri* (Munro)
[*A. palmaris* (Whitley)]
Allotarius spariformis (Ogilby)
**Chrysophrys auratus* (Schneider)
Mylio latus (Houttuyn)
Rhabdosargus sarba (Forsskal)
Taius tumifrons (Temminck &
  Schlegel)

SCIAENIDAE

**Argyrosomus hololepidotus* (Lacépède)
Collinichthys novaeguineae Nichols
Johnieops sina (Cuvier)
Johnius dussumieri (Cuvier)
Kathala axillaris (Cuvier)
Otolithes argenteus (Cuvier)
Protonibea diacanthus (Lacépède)

MULLIDAE

Parupeneus barberinoides (Bleeker)
P. bifasciatus (Lacépède)
P. chrysopleuron (Schlegel)
P. cyclostomus (Lacépède)
P. fraterculus Valenciennes
P. heptacanthus Lacépède
P. indicus Shaw
P. luteus Valenciennes
P. multifasciatus Bleeker
P. pleurostigma (Bennett)
**Upeneichthys lineatus* (Bloch &
  Schneider)
U. sp.
Upeneus moluccensis (Bleeker)
U. sulphureus Cuvier
U. sundaicus Bleeker
U. tragula Richardson
U. vittatus Lacépède

MONODACTYLIDAE

Monodactylus argenteus (Linnaeus)
[*Schuettea woodwardi* (Waite)]

PEMPHERIDAE

Leptobrama mulleri Steindachner
**Parapriacanthus elongatus*
  (McCulloch)
P. ransonneti (Steindachner)
P. unwini (Ogilby)
Pempheris analis Waite
**P. klunzingeri* McCulloch
**P. multiradiata* Klunzinger
P. oualensis Cuvier
P. schwenkii Bleeker
P. spp. (2)

TOXOTIDAE

Toxotes chatareus (Hamilton)
T. jaculator (Pallas)

KYPHOSIDAE

[**Girella tephraeops* (Richardson)]
**G. zebra* (Richardson)
Kyphosus gibsoni (Ogilby)
[*K. cornelii* (Whitley)]
**K. sydneyanus* (Günther)
K. vaigiensis (Quoy & Gaimard)

EPHIPPIDAE

Drepane punctata (Linnaeus)
Platax batavianus Cuvier
P. pinnatus (Linnaeus)
P. tiera (Forsskal)
Zabidius novemaculeatus (McCulloch)

SCATOPHAGIDAE

Scatophagus argus (Bloch)
Selenotoca multifasciatus (Richardson)

SCORPIDIDAE

Microcanthus strigatus (Cuvier)
[**Neatypus obliquus* Waite]
**Scorpis aequipinnis* Richardson
**S. georgianus* Valenciennes
**Tilodon sexfasciatum* (Richardson)

CHAETODONTIDAE

Chaetodon adiergastos Seale
[*C. assarius* Waite]

C. *aureofasciatus* Macleay
C. *auriga* Forsskal
C. *citrinellus* Cuvier
C. *ephippium* Cuvier
C. *kleini* Bloch
C. *lineolatus* Cuvier
C. *lunula* (Lacépède)
C. *meyeri* Schneider
C. *ornatissimus* Cuvier
C. *plebeius* Cuvier
C. *punctatofasciatus* Cuvier
C. *speculum* Cuvier
C. *trifascialis* Quoy & Gaimard
C. *trifasciatus* (Park)
C. *ulietensis* Cuvier
C. *unimaculatus* Bloch
Chelmon marginalis Richardson
Chelmonops truncatus (Kner)
Coradion chrysozonus (Cuvier)
Forcipiger flavissimus Jordan &
    McGregor
Heniochus acuminatus (Linnaeus)
H. *chrysostomus* Cuvier
H. *diphreutes* Jordan
H. *singularius* Smith & Radcliffe
H. *varius* (Cuvier)
Parachaetodon ocellatus (Cuvier)

POMACANTHIDAE

Apolemichthys trimaculatus (Cuvier)
Centropyge bicolor (Bloch)
C. *eibli* Klausewitz
C. *tibicen* (Cuvier)
Chaetodontoplus duboulayi (Günther)
C. *personifer* (McCulloch)
Euxiphipops navarchus (Cuvier)
E. *sexstriatus* (Cuvier)
Pomacanthus imperator (Bloch)
P. *semicirculatus* (Cuvier)
Pygoplites diacanthus (Boddaert)

ENOPLOSIDAE

Enoplosus armatus (White)

PENTACEROTIDAE

Histiopterus typus (Temminck &
    Schlegel)
Paristiopterus gallipavo Whitley
[*Parazanclistius hutchinsi* Hardy]
Pentaceropsis recurvirostris
    (Richardson)
Pseudopentaceros richardsoni (Smith)

Zanclistius elevatus (Ramsay &
    Ogilby)

OPLEGNATHIDAE

Oplegnathus woodwardi (Waite)

POMACENTRIDAE

Abudefduf bengalensis (Bloch)
A. *saxatilis* (Linnaeus)
A. *septemfasciatus* (Cuvier)
A. *sexfasciatus* (Lacépède)
A. *sordidus* (Forsskal)
Amblyglyphidodon curacao (Bloch)
Amphiprion clarkii (Bennett)
A. *ocellaris* Cuvier
A. *perideraion* Bleeker
A. *rubrocinctus* Richardson
A. *sandaracinos* Allen
Cheiloprion labiatus (Day)
Chromis atripectoralis Schultz &
    Welander
C. *caerulea* (Cuvier)
C. *cinerascens* (Cuvier)
C. *fumea* (Tanaka)
[*C. *klunzingeri* Whitley]
C. *margaritifer* Fowler
[C. *megalopsis* Allen]
C. *weberi* Fowler & Bean
[*C. *westaustralis* Allen]
Dascyllus aruanus (Linnaeus)
D. *reticulatus* (Richardson)
D. *trimaculatus* (Rüppell)
Dischistodus fasciatus (Cuvier)
D. *prosopotaenia* (Bleeker)
Hemiglyphidodon plagiometopon
    Bleeker
N. *azysron* (Bleeker)
N. *cyanomos* (Bleeker)
Neopomacentrus filamentosus (Macleay)
Paraglyphidodon melas (Cuvier)
P. *nigroris* (Cuvier)
[*Parma bicolor* Allen & Larson]
[*P. *mccullochi* Whitley]
[*P. *occidentalis* Allen & Hoese]
*P. *victoriae* (Günther)
Plectroglyphidodon dickii (Liénard)
P. *johnstonianus* Fowler & Ball
P. *lacrymatus* (Quoy & Gaimard)
P. *leucozonus* (Bleeker)
Pomacentrus alexanderae Evermann
    & Seale
P. *amboinensis* Bleeker
P. *coelestis* Jordan & Starks
P. *milleri* Taylor

P. *moluccensis* (Bleeker)
P. *vaiuli* Jordan & Seale
P. sp.
Pristotis jerdoni (Day)
Stegastes fasciolatus (Ogilby)
S. *lividus* (Bloch & Schneider)
S. *nigricans* (Lacépède)
S. *obreptus* (Whitley)

CIRRHITIDAE

Amblycirrhitus bimacula (Jenkins)
Cirrhitichthys aprinus (Cuvier)
C. *oxycephalus* (Bleeker)
Cyprinocirrhites polyactis (Bleeker)
Paracirrhites arcatus (Cuvier)
P. *forsteri* (Bloch & Schneider)
P. *hemistictus* (Günther)

CHIRONEMIDAE

Chironemus georgianus Cuvier
Threpterius maculosus Richardson

APLODACTYLIDAE

[*Dactylosargus* sp.]

CHEILODACTYLIDAE

[*Cheilodactylus gibbosus* Richardson]
*C. *nigripes* Richardson
[*C. *rubrolabiatus* Allen & Heemstra]
Dactylophora nigricans (Richardson)
Nemadactylus macropterus (Schneider)
*N. *valenciennesi* (Whitley)

LATRIDAE

Latris lineata (Bloch & Schneider)

CEPOLIDAE

Acanthocepola abbreviata
    (Valenciennes)

MUGILIDAE

Aldrichetta forsteri (Valenciennes)
Liza argentea (Quoy & Gaimard)
L. *subviridis* (Valenciennes)
L. *vaigiensis* (Quoy & Gaimard)
Mugil cephalus Linnaeus
Myxus elongatus (Günther)
Valamugil buchanani (Bleeker)

SPHYRAENIDAE

Sphyraena barracuda (Walbaum)
S. flavipinnis
S. helleri Jenkins
S. jello Cuvier
*S. novaehollandae Günther
S. obtusata Cuvier

POLYNEMIDAE

Eleutheronema tetradactylum (Shaw)
Polynemus auratus (McKay)
P. intermedius Nichols
P. macrochir Günther
P. nigripinnis (Munro)
P. plebius Broussonet
P. specularis De Vis

LABRIDAE

Achoerodus gouldii (Richardson)
Anampses caeruleopunctatus Rüppell
A. geographicus Valenciennes
[A. lennardi Scott]
A. meleagrides Valenciennes
*Austrolabrus maculatus (Macleay)
Bodianus axillaris (Bennett)
B. bilunulatus (Lacépède)
*B. frenchii (Klunzinger)
B. perdito (Quoy & Gaimard)
B. vulpinus (Richardson)
Cheilinus chlorurus (Bloch)
C. fasciatus (Bloch)
C. rhodochrous Günther
C. trilobatus Lacépède
Cheilio inermis (Forsskal)
Choerodon cyanodus (Richardson)
C. cephalotes (Castelnau)
C. jordani (Snyder)
[C. rubescens (Günther)]
C. schoenleini (Valenciennes)
C. vitta Ogilby
C. spp. (2)
Cirrhilabrus temmincki Bleeker
[Conniella apterygia Allen]
[*Coris auricularis (Valenciennes)]
C. aygula Lacépède
C. caudimacula Quoy & Gaimard
C. gaimardi (Quoy & Gaimard)
C. pictoides Randall & Kuiter
Cymolutes praetextata (Quoy &
  Gaimard)
*Dotalabrus aurantiacus (Castelnau)
[*D. sp.]
Epibulus insidiator (Pallas)

*Eupetrichthys angustipes Ramsay &
  Ogilby
Gomphosus varius (Lacépède)
Halichoeres bimaculatus Rüppell
H. biocellatus Schultz
[*H. brownfieldi (Whitley)]
H. centriquadrus (Lacépède)
H. margaritaceous (Valenciennes)
H. marginatus Rüppell
H. melanochir Fowler & Bean
H. nigrescens Bleeker
H. nebulosus (Valenciennes)
H. trimaculatus Rüppell
Hemigymnus fasciatus (Bloch)
H. melapterus (Bloch)
Hologymnosus semidiscus (Lacépède)
Labrichthys unilineatus (Guichenot)
Labroides bicolor Fowler & Bean
L. dimidiatus (Valenciennes)
Leptojulis cyanopleura (Bleeker)
Macropharyngodon ornatus Randall
M. negrosensis Herre
Novaculichthys taeniorus (Lacépède)
*Ophthalmolepis lineolatus
  (Valenciennes)
*Pictilabrus laticlavius (Richardson)
[*P. sp.]
Pseudojuloides elongatus Ayling &
  Russell
Pseudocheilinus hexataenia (Bleeker)
[*Pseudolabrus biserialis (Klunzinger)]
*P. parilus (Richardson)
Pteragogus flagellifera (Valenciennes)
Stethojulis bandanensis (Bleeker)
S. interrupta (Bleeker)
S. strigiventer (Bennett)
[*Suezichthys sp.]
Thalassoma amblycephalus (Bleeker)
T. hardwickei (Bennett)
T. janseni (Bleeker)
T. lunare (Linneaus)
T. lutescens (Lay & Bennett)
T. purpureum (Forsskal)
[T. septemfasciata Scott]
Xenojulis margaritaceous (Macleay)
Xyrichthys sp.

ODACIDAE

*Haletta semifasciatus (Valenciennes)
*Neoodax balteatus (Valenciennes)
*Odax acroptilus (Richardson)
*O. cyanomelas (Richardson)
*Siphonognathus argyrophanes
  Richardson
*S. attenuatus (Ogilby)

*S. beddomei (Johnson)
*S. caninus Scott
*S. radiatus (Quoy & Gaimard)
*S. sp.

SCARIDAE

Bolbometopon muricatum
  (Valenciennes)
Cetoscarus bicolor (Rüppell)
Leptoscarus vaigiensis (Quoy &
  Gaimard)
Scarus frenatus Lacépède
S. ghobban Forsskal
S. globiceps Valenciennes
S. janthinochir Bleeker
S. oedema (Snyder)
S. oviceps Valenciennes
S. psittacus Forsskal
S. rivulatus Valenciennes
S. rubroviolaceus (Bleeker)
S. schlegeli (Bleeker)
S. sordidus Forsskal

OPISTOGNATHIDAE

Opistognathus darwiniensis Macleay
[O. inornatus Ramsay & Ogilby]
[O. reticulatus (McKay)]
[O. sp.]
O. sp.

MUGILOIDIDAE

*Parapercis allporti (Günther)
[P. biordinis Allen]
P. cephalopunctata (Seale)
P. clathrata Ogilby
P. diplospilus Gomon
*P. haackei (Steindachner)
[*P. naevosa Serventy]
P nebulosa (Quoy & Gaimard)
*P. ramsayi Steindachner
P. sp.

PERCOPHIDIDAE

Bembrops aethalea McKay
B. indica McKay
Branchiopsaron ozawai McKay
Chironema chlorotaenia McKay
*Enigmapercis reducta Whitley

TRICHONOTIDAE

Trichonotus setiger Bloch & Schneider

CREEDIDAE

[*Creedia alleni Nelson]
 Limnichthys fasciatus Waite
 Squamicreedia obtusata Rendahl

LEPTOSCOPIDAE

*Crapatalus arenarius McCulloch

URANOSCOPIDAE

[*Ichthyscopus barbatus Mees]
 [I. insperatus Mees]
*I. sannio Whitley
 [I. spinosus Mees]
*Kathetostoma sp.
*K. nigrofasciatum Waite &
 McCulloch
 Uranoscopus cognatus Cantor

CHAMPSODONTIDAE

*Champsodon vorax Günther

BLENNIIDAE

Aspidontus dussumieri (Valenciennes)
A. taeniatus Quoy & Gaimard
Atrosalarias fuscus holomelas
 (Günther)
Cirripectes filamentosus Alleyne &
 Macleay
C. sebae (Valenciennes)
[C. sp.]
Ecsenius bicolor (Day)
E. lineatus Klausewitz
E. oculus Springer
E. yaeyamaensis (Aoyagi)
Entomacrodus decussatus (Bleeker)
E. striatus (Quoy & Gaimard)
Exallias brevis (Kner)
Herculops cornifer (Rüppell)
Istiblennius chrysospilos (Bleeker)
I. edentulus (Bloch & Schneider)
I. lineatus (Valenciennes)
I. meleagris (Valenciennes)
I. periophthalmus (Valenciennes)
Laiphognathus multimaculatus Smith
Meiacanthus grammistes
 (Valenciennes)
Mimoblennius atrocinctus Smith-Vaniz
 & Springer
Omobranchus ferox (Herre)
O. germaini (Sauvage)

O. lineolatus (Kner)
O. punctatus (Valenciennes)
*Parablennius sp.
Petroscirtes breviceps Valenciennes
P. mitratus Rüppell
Plagiotremus rhinorhynchus (Bleeker)
P. tapeinosoma (Klunzinger)
Salarias fasciatus (Bloch)
S. sexfilum Günther
S. spaldingi Macleay
S. sp.
Stanulus talboti Springer
Xiphasia setifer Swainson

CONGROGADIDAE

Blennodesmus scapularis Günther
Congrogadus subducens Richardson
Congrogadoides malayanus Weber

NOTOGRAPTIDAE

Notograptus gregoryi Whitley
N. guttatus Günther
N. livingstonei Whitley

TRIPTERYGIIDAE

*Brachynectes fasciatus Scott
*Helcogramma decurrens McCulloch
 & Waite
 H. spp. (2)
*Lepidoblennius marmoratus
 (Macleay)
 Norfolkia brachylepis (Schultz)
*N. macleayanus (Lucas)
 N. spp.(3)
 Vauclusella spp. (6)
*Verconectes bucephalus (McCulloch
 & Waite)

CLINIDAE

*Cristiceps aurantiacus Castelnau
*C. australis Valenciennes
*C. sp.
*Heteroclinus adelaidae Castelnau
*H. eckloniae (McKay)
*H. equiradiatus (Milward)
*H. forsteri (Castelnau)
*H. heptaeolus (Ogilby)
*H. macrophthalmus Hoese
*H. roseus (Günther)
*H. spp. (5)
[*Ophiclinops hutchinsi George &
 Springer]

*O. varius (McCulloch & Waite)
*Ophiclinus brevipinnis George &
 Springer
*O. antarcticus (Castelnau)
*O. gracilis Waite
*O. ningulus George & Springer
[*O. pectoralis George & Springer]
*Peronedys anguillaris Steindachner
*Sticharium dorsale (Günther)
*S. clarkae George & Springer

CALLIONYMIDAE

Callionymus belcheri Richardson
*C. calcaratus Macleay
 C. enneactis Bleeker
[*C. goodladi (Whitley)]
 C. grossi McCulloch
 C. limiceps Ogilby
 C. moretonensis Johnson
 C. sagittus Pallas
 C. sublaevis McCulloch
 Dactylopus dactylopus (Valenciennes)
 Diplogrammus xenicus (Jordan &
 Thompson)
 Liopsaron insolitum McKay
*Synchiropus calauropomus
 Richardson
 S. morrisoni (Schultz)
*S. papilio (Günther)
*S. phasis Günther
 S. picturatus (Peters)
 S. rameus (McCulloch)

GOBIIDAE

Acentrogobius gracilis (Bleeker)
A. janthinopterus (Bleeker)
Amblyeleotris fasciata (Herre)
A. periophthalmus (Bleeker)
A. wheeleri Polunin & Lubbock
Amblygobius decussatus (Bleeker)
A. phalaena (Valenciennes)
A. sp.
Apocryptodon madurensis Bleeker
*Arenigobius bifrenatus (Kner)
Asterropteryx semipunctatus (Rüppell)
Bathygobius fuscus (Rüppell)
B. laddi
Boleophthalmus pectinirostris
 (Linnaeus)
Cabillus lacertops Smith
Callogobius hasseltii (Bleeker)
C. liolepis Koumans
*C. mucosus (Günther)
C. sclateri (Steindachner)
C. snelliusi Koumans

Cryptocentrus caeruleomaculatus (Herre)
C. cebuanus Herre
C. cinctus (Herre)
C. fasciatus (Playfair)
C. obliquus (Herre)
C. spp. (2)
Ctenogobiops sp.
[**Eviota bimaculata* Lachner & Karanella]
E. infulata (Smith)
[**E. inutilis* Whitley]
E. melasma Lachner & Karanella
E. queenslandica Whitley
E. storthynx Herre
E. zebrina Lachner & Karanella
E. zonura Jordan & Seale
E. spp. (3)
Favonigobius exquisitus Whitley
*F. lateralis (Macleay)
*F. suppositus (Sauvage)
F. sp.
Fusigobius spp. (3)
Glossogobius giurus (Hamilton)
Gnatholepis inconsequens Whitley
Gobiodon citrinus (Rüppell)
G. histrio (Valenciennes)
G. quinquestrigatus Bleeker
Gobiopsis bravoi (Herre)
Istigobius decoratus (Herre)
I. ornatus (Rüppell)
I. perspicillatus (Herre)
I. spence (Smith)
Mugilogobius platystoma (Günther)
Nesogobius pulchellus (Castelnau)
*N. spp. (2)
Oplopomus oplopomus (Valenciennes)
Oxyurichthys sp.
Pandaka lidwilli (McCulloch)
Parachaeturichthys polynema (Bleeker)
Paragobiodon echinocephalus (Rüppell)
P. lacunicolus (Kendall & Goldsborough)
Parioglossus taeniatus Regan
Periophthalmus koelreuteri (Pallas)
P. regius Whitley
Periophthalmodon schlosseri (Pallas)
Priolepis cinctus (Regan)
P. nuchifasciatus (Günther)
P. semidoliatus (Valenciennes)
Pseudogobius javanicus (Bleeker)
*P. olorum (Sauvage)
*P. sp.
Ptereleotris evides Jordans & Hubbs
Scartelaos histiophorus (Valenciennes)
Silhouettea insinuans Smith

Tridentiger trigonocephalus (Gill)
Trimma okinawae
T. sp.
Valenciennea immaculatus (Ni Yong)
V. longipinnis (Bennett)
V. muralis (Valenciennes)
V. puellaris (Tomiyama)
V. sp.
Vanderhorstia ornatissimus Smith
Vireosa hanae Jordan & Snyder
Yongeichthys nebulosus (Forsskal)

ELEOTRIDAE

Bostrichthys sinensis (Lacépède)
Butis amboinensis (Bleeker)
B. butis (Hamilton)
Prionobutis microps (Weber)

GOBIOIDIDAE

Brachyamblyopus coecus (Weber)
B. rubristriatus (Saville-Kent)

KURTIDAE

Kurtus gulliveri Castelnau

ACANTHURIDAE

Acanthurus bleekeri Günther
A. dussumieri Valenciennes
A. glaucopareius Cuvier
A. grammoptilus Richardson
A. lineatus (Linnaeus)
A. nigrofuscus (Forsskal)
A. olivaceous Bloch & Schneider
A. triostegus (Linnaeus)
Ctenochaetus strigosus (Bennett)
Naso brevirostris (Valenciennes)
N. lituratus (Bloch & Schneider)
N. tuberosus Lacépède
N. unicornis (Forsskal)
Zebrasoma scopas (Valenciennes)
Z. veliferum (Bloch)

ZANCLIDAE

Zanclus cornutus (Linnaeus)

SIGANIDAE

Siganus canaliculatus (Park)
S. doliatus (Valenciennes)
S. fuscescens (Houttuyn)
S. lineatus (Linnaeus)
S. punctatus (Schneider)

[*S. trispilos* Woodland & Allen]
S. unimaculatus (Evermann & Seale)
S. vermiculatus (Valenciennes)

GEMPYLIDAE

*Leionura atun (Euphrasen)
*Rexea solandri (Cuvier)
*Ruvettus tydemani Weber

TRICHIURIDAE

*Assurger anzac (Alexander)
Lepturacanthus savala (Cuvier)
*Trichiurus coxii Ramsay & Ogilby

SCOMBRIDAE

Acanthocybium solandri (Cuvier)
*Allothunnus fallai Serventy
Auxis rochei (Risso)
A. thazard (Lacépède)
Cybiosarda elegans (Whitley)
Euthynnus affinis (Cantor)
*Gasterochisma melampus Richardson
Grammatorcynus bicarinatus (Quoy & Gaimard)
G. bilineatus (Rüppell)
Gymnosarda unicolor (Rüppell)
Katsuwonus pelamis (Linnaeus)
Rastrelliger kanagurta (Cuvier)
Sarda orientalis (Temminck & Schlegel)
*Scomber australasicus Cuvier
Scomberomorus commerson (Lacépède)
S. munroi Collette & Russo
S. queenslandicus Munro
S. semifasciatus (Macleay)
Thunnus alalunga (Bonnaterre)
T. albacares (Bonnaterre)
*T. maccoyii (Castelnau)
T. obesus (Lowe)
T. tonggol (Bleeker)

XIPHIIDAE

Xiphias gladius Linnaeus

ISTIOPHORIDAE

Istiophorus platypterus (Shaw & Nodder)
Makaira audax (Philippi)
M. indica (Cuvier)
M. mazara (Jordan & Snyder)
Tetrapturus angustirostris Tanaka

CENTROLOPHIDAE

*Hyperoglyphe porosa (Richardson)
Psenopsis humerosus Munro
P. sp.

MALACANTHIDAE

Malacanthus brevirostris Bleeker

NOMEIDAE

Nomeus albula (Meuschen)
Psenes spp. (2)

PSETTODIDAE

Psettodes erumei (Bloch & Schneider)

BOTHIDAE

Arnoglossus aspilos Whitley
A. intermedius (Bleeker)
*A. muelleri (Klunzinger)
Bothus pantherinus (Rüppell)
Grammatobothus polyophthalmus
  (Bleeker)
Pseudorhombus anomalus Ogilby
P. arsius (Hamilton)
P. dupliciocellatus Regan
P. elevatus Ogilby
P. jenynsii (Bleeker)
P. spinosus McCulloch

PLEURONECTIDAE

*Ammotretis elongatus McCulloch
*A. rostratus Günther
*Azygopus pinnifasciatus Norman
Brachypleura novaezealandiae
  Günther
Psammodiscus ocellatus Günther
*Rhombosolea tapirina Günther
Samaris cacatuae (Ogilby)

SOLEIDAE

Achlyopa nigra (Macleay)
Aesopia heterorhinos (Bleeker)
A. microcephalus (Günther)
*Aseraggodes haackeanus
  (Steindachner)
A. melanostictus (Peters)
Brachirus aspilos (Bleeker)
Dexillichthys muelleri (Steindachner)
Liachirus melanospilus (Bleeker)

L. whitleyi Chabanaud
Pardachirus pavoninus (Lacépède)
Phyllichthys punctatus McCulloch
Rendahlia jaubertensis (Rendahl)
Strabozebrias cancellatus (McCulloch)
S. munroi (Whitley)
*Synaptura hediste Mees
Zebrias craticula (McCulloch)
Z. quagga (Kaup)

CYNOGLOSSIDAE

Cynoglossus bilineatus (Lacépède)
*C. broadhursti Waite
C. maculipinnis Rendahl
C. punticeps (Richardson)
Paraplagusia acuminata Castelnau
P. guttata (Macleay)
P. unicolor (Macleay)

TRIACANTHIDAE

Triacanthus biaculeatus (Bloch)
Tripodichthys blochi (Bleeker)

TRIACANTHODIDAE

Halimochirugus alcocki Weber
H. centriscoides Alcock
Macrorhamphosodes platycheilus
  Fowler
Paratriacanthodes retrospinus Fowler

BALISTIDAE

Balistapus undulatus (Park)
Balistoides viridescens (Bloch &
  Schneider)
Melichthys vidua (Solander)
Pseudobalistes fuscus (Bloch &
  Schneider)
Rhinecanthus aculeatus (Linnaeus)
R. rectangulus (Bloch & Schneider)
Sufflamen bursa (Bloch & Schneider)
S. chrysopterus (Bloch & Schneider)
S. fraenatus Latreille

MONACANTHIDAE

Compiled by J.B. Hutchins, Western
Australian Museum

*Acanthaluteres spilomelanurus (Quoy
  & Gaimard)
Alutera monoceros (Linnaeus)
A. scripta (Osbeck)

Anacanthus barbatus (Gray)
*Bigener brownii (Richardson)
*Brachaluteres jacksonianus (Quoy &
  Gaimard)
Cantherhines dumerili (Hollard)
C. fronticinctus (Günther)
C. pardalis (Rüppell)
*Cantheschenia longipinnis (Fraser-
  Brunner)
Chaetoderma pencilligera (Cuvier)
[Colurodontis paxmani Hutchins]
*Eubalichthys bucephalus (Whitley)
[E. caeruleoguttatus Hutchins]
*E. mosaicus (Ramsay & Ogilby)
*E. sp.
*Meuschenia flavolineata Hutchins
*M. freycineti (Quoy & Gaimard)
*M. galii (Waite)
*M. hippocrepis (Quoy & Gaimard)
*M. venusta Hutchins
Monacanthus chinensis (Osbeck)
*Nelusetta ayraudi (Quoy & Gaimard)
Oxymonacanthus longirostris (Bloch
  & Schneider)
Paramonacanthus filicauda (Günther)
P. japonicus (Tilesius)
P. sp.
*Parika scaber (Forster)
*Penicipelta vittiger (Castelnau)
Pervagor janthinosoma (Bleeker)
Pseudomonacanthus elongatus Fraser-
  Brunner
P. peroni (Hollard)
*Scobinichthys granulatus (Shaw)
Stephanolepis auratus (Castelnau)
Thamnaconus hypargyreus (Cope)
T. modestoides (Barnard)
T. striatus (Kotthaus)
T. tesselatus (Günther)

OSTRACIONTIDAE

*Anoplocapros grayi (Kaup)
*A. lenticularis (Richardson)
*Aracana aurita (Shaw & Nodder)
*A. ornata (Gray)
*Caprichthys gymnura McCulloch &
  Waite
*Capropygia unistriata Kaup
Lactoria cornuta (Linnaeus)
L. diaphana (Bloch & Schneider)
Ostracion cubicus Linnaeus
O. meleagris Shaw
*Paracanthostracion pentacanthus
  (Bleeker)
Rhynchostracion nasus (Bloch)

R. rhinorhynchus (Bleeker)
*Strophiurichthys robustus Fraser-
   Brunner
*S. sp.
*Tetrosomus gibbosus (Linnaeus)
*Trioris reipublicae (Ogilby)

TETRAODONTIDAE

Amblyrhynchotes sp.
Arothron hispidus (Linnaeus)
A. immaculatus (Bloch & Schneider)
A. nigropunctatus (Bloch &
   Schneider)
A. stellatus (Bloch & Schneider)
Canthigaster coronatus (Vaillant &
   Sauvage)

C. janthinopterus (Bleeker)
C. rivulatus (Schlegel)
Chelonodon patoca (Hamilton)
*Contusus brevicaudus Hardy
Lagocephalus lunaris (Bloch &
   Schneider)
L. sceleratus (Gmelin)
L. spadiceus (Richardson)
Marilyna darwinii (Castelnau)
M. meraukensis (De Beaufort)
*Omegophora armilla (McCulloch &
   Waite)
[*O. cyanopunctata Hardy &
   Hutchins]
Polyspina piosae (Whitley)
Sphoeroides multistriatus (Richardson)
S. oblongus (Bloch)

Torquigener pallimaculatus Hardy
[T. paxtoni Hardy]
*T. pleurogramma (Regan)
[*T. vicinus Whitley]
T. whitleyi (Paradice)

TRIODONTIDAE

Triodon macropterus Lesson

DIODONTIDAE

*Allomycterus pilatus Whitley
Chilomycterus affinis (Günther)
C. orbicularis (Bloch)
Diodon holacanthus Linnaeus
D. liturosus Shaw
*D. nicthemerus Cuvier

Index

The following index contains entries for subject matter and illustrations contained in this book and its companion volumes, *Pacific Marine Fishes*, 1-8. Some of the names used in earlier volumes of this series, however, have been revised to reflect an updated or otherwise changed nomenclatural standing; all such names listed in text and index of these volumes are listed in this index but are referenced to show the revised identifications.

Aeoliscus strigatus, **320, 321, 1416, 1417**
Aesopia, 1099
Aesopia heterorhinos (See *Soleichthys heterorhinos*)
Aetapcus maculatus, **2221**
Aethaloperca rogaa, **646**
Aetobatus, 1672
Aetobatus narinari, **1076,** 1077, **1671, 1672,** 1672
Aetomylaeus, 1077
AGONIDAE, 2165
Agonus acipenserinus, 2165, **2167**
Aholeholes, 308
Alabes parvulus, **2264**
Albula vulpes, **1043**
Aldrichetta forsteri, 2235, **2389**
Alectis ciliaris, **1050**
Alectis indica, **426, 1050, 1051,** 2227, **2336**
Alectis major, **1051**
ALEPISAURIDAE, 1257
Alepisaurus borealis, **1256**
Alepisaurus ferox, 1257
Alfoncinos, **548,** 1161
Alloclinus holderi, **2092**
Allomycterus pilatus, 2246
Aluterus, 1905, 2245
Aluterus monoceros, **125**
Aluterus scriptus, 122, **1356, 1632, 1633, 1906, 2177**
Amanses scopas, **1350, 1351, 1631**
AMARSIPIDAE, 1220
AMBASSIDAE, 2223
Ambassis interrupta, **2297**
Ambassis sp., **1430**
Amblyapistus taenianotus, **517, 962, 1624**
Amblycirrhitus, 155, 660
Amblycirrhitus bimacula, **1142**
Amblyeleotris fasciata, **1895**
Amblyeleotris guttata, **1601**
Amblyeleotris periophthalmus, **2459**
Amblyeleotris randalli, **1601**
Amblyeleotris rhyax, **1601**
Amblyeleotris wheeleri, **2458**
Amblygaster leiogaster, **2259**
Amblyglyphidodon, 2234
Amblyglyphidodon aureus, **305, 1564**
Amblyglyphidodon curacao, **1023**
Amblyglyphidodon leucogaster, **200, 304, 1558**
Amblygobius, 2242
Amblygobius albimaculatus, **634, 635**
Amblygobius decussatus, **1600, 1894**
Amblygobius phalaena, **1602, 2463**
Amblygobius rainfordi, **1896**
Amniataba caudavittatus, 2225, **2319**
Amora, 219
Amphichaetodon melbae, **2019**
Amphiprion, 181
Amphiprion akindynos, **288, 292, 1547,**

1698, 1699, 1700, 1701, 1702, 1704
Amphiprion allardi, 701, **705, 708**
Amphiprion biaculeatus (See *Premnas biaculeatus*)
Amphiprion chrysopterus, **191, 296, 297, 1019, 1551**
Amphiprion clarkii, **180, 183, 185, 292, 704, 708, 709, 714, 715, 1018, 1019, 1547, 1548, 1551**
Amphiprion ephippium, 292
Amphiprion frenatus, **184, 186, 187, 1020, 1021**
Amphiprion latezonatus, **289**
Amphiprion laticlavius (See *Amphiprion polymnus*)
Amphiprion melanopus, **293, 1545, 1551, 1552, 1696, 1697,** 2234
Amphiprion nigripes, **561,** 701, **710, 711, 712, 713, 714**
Amphiprion ocellaris, **188, 189, 298, 299, 300, 301, 1021**
Amphiprion percula, 188
Amphiprion perideraion, **182, 185, 294, 295, 1017,** 1545, **1548, 1549, 1550, 1703, 1704, 1705**
Amphiprion polymnus, **183**
Amphiprion rubrocinctus, 2234, **2372**
Amphiprion sandaracinos, 188
Amphiprion tricinctus, **290, 291**
Amphiprion xanthurus, **180**
Amphiprion sp., **287, 706, 707**
Amphistichus argenteus, 2029, **2029**
Amphistichus rhodoterus, 2029, **2030**
Amphotistius kuhli, **1394, 1395,** 2214
Anago anago, **352**
Anampses caeruleopunctatus, **144, 145, 440, 623, 878, 2401**
Anampses chrysocephalus, **440**
Anampses cuvieri, **445**
Anampses lennardi, 2237, **2402**
Anampses meleagrides, **442, 864, 2401**
Anampses neoguinaicus, **142, 863**
Anampses rubrocaudatus (See *Anampses chrysocephalus*)
Anampses twistii, **440, 863**
ANARHICHADIDAE, 2103
Anarhichas, 2103
Anarrhichthys, 2103
Anarrhichthys ocellatus, 2103, **2103, 2104**
Anchovies, 1951
Anemonefishes, 181, 289, 701, 1545
Angelfishes, 7, 39, 781, 2232
Angel sharks, 1069
Anglerfishes, 258, 2218
Anguilla, 260
Anguilla japonica, **351**
ANGUILLIFORMES, 2214
Anisotremus davidsoni, **2005**
Anisotremus taeniatus, **2004**
ANOMALOPIDAE, 1411
Anomalops, 1411
Anomalops katoptron, **1411**
Anoplarchus purpurescens, 2100
Anoplocapros lenticularis, 2246,

2494
Anoplopoma fimbria, 2148, **2148**
ANOPLOPOMATIDAE, 2148
ANTENNARIIDAE, 258, 2218
Antennarius, 259
Antennarius avalonis, **1959**
Antennarius biocellatus, **1365**
Antennarius chironectes (See *A. pictus*)
Antennarius coccineus, **529, 828**
Antennarius indicus, **529**
Antennarius maculatus, **530, 1910**
Antennarius nox, 259
Antennarius nummifer, **528,** 2218, **2265**
Antennarius phymatodes (See *A. maculatus*)
Antennarius pictus, **528, 529**
Antennarius sanguifluus, 259
Antennarius sanguineus, **1960, 1961**
Antennarius striatus, 259, **270, 532, 1910**
Antennarius strigatus, **1959**
Antennarius tridens (See *A. striatus*)
Antennarius trisignatus, **528**
Anthias, 643, 2223
Anthias fasciatus, **239**
Anthias hutchi, **1469, 1471**
Anthias kashiwae, **2304**
Anthias pleurotaenia, **1467, 1468, 1470**
Anthias rubrizonatus, **2303**
Anthias squamipinnis, **489, 490, 649, 1224, 1467, 1857, 1858-9, 1860, 1861**
Anthias sp., **646, 742, 760, 1467**
Anthiinae, 489, 2223
Anyperodon, 643
Anyperodon leucogrammicus, **491, 647, 1851**
Aphareus, 675
Aphareus furcatus, **675, 1293**
Apistus carinatus, **533**
APLODACTYLIDAE, 2235
Apodes, 260
Apogon, 241, 678, 1681
Apogon angustatus, **687, 2330**
Apogon apogonides, **463**
Apogon aroubiensis, **1430, 1436, 1683**
Apogon aureus, **966, 1447, 1678**
Apogon chrysotaenia, **2331**
Apogon coccineus, **463,** 2226, **2320**
Apogon compressus, **1434, 1435**
Apogon cooki, **2320**
Apogon crassiceps, 2226, **2323**
Apogon cyanosoma, **243, 679, 967, 1434, 1435**
Apogon darnleyensis, **2322**
Apogon doederleini, **1682, 2321**
Apogon dovii, **1994**
Apogon endekataenia, **686, 687**
Apogon erythrinus (See *A. coccineus*)
Apogon exostigma, **463**
Apogon fasciatus, **460**
Apogon fraenatus, **460, 1439**
Apogon fragilis, **1442, 1685**
Apogon hartzfeldi, **1437, 1683, 2322**
Apogon kallopterus, **685,** 686, **1438**

Bothus pantherinus, **2482**
Bothus sp., **1095**
Boxfishes, 114, 2177, 2245
Brachaluteres, 2245
Brachaluteres jacksonianus, **2489**
Brachirus (See *Dendrochirus*)
Brachyamblyopus coecus, 2242, **2478**
Brachyistius frenatus, 2029, **2031**
Brachysomophis cirrhocheilos, **2258**
Brama brama, 1171, 1173
Brama japonica, 1171, 1172, 1173
Brama sp., **1170**
BRAMIDAE, 1170
BRANCHIOSTEGIDAE, 531
Branchiostegus argentatus, **532**
Branchiostegus japonicus, **533**
Brosmichthys marginata, **1962**
Brotula multibarbata, **1604,** 2218, **2269**
Brotulids, 997
Bulbonaricus brauni, **2280**
Bullseyes, 1254, 2230
Butterfishes, 416, 1220
Butterfly-bream, 666, 1493
Butterflyfishes, 39, 743, 1520, 2232
BYTHITIDAE, 2218

C
Caesio, 221, 673, **742**
Caesio caerulaureus, **677, 1296**
Caesio chrysozonus, **223, 1296, 1503,** **1872, 1873, 2340**
Caesio erythrogaster, **1502, 1872**
Caesio pisang, **1503**
Caesio pulcherrimus, **1505**
Caesio tile, **676, 1295, 1502, 1504**
Caesio xanthonotus, **676, 1294**
CAESIONIDAE, 2227
Caesioperca rasor, **2305**
CAESIOSCORPIDAE, 2227
Calamus brachysomus, **2007**
Callanthias japonicus, **1224**
CALLIONYMIDAE, 219, 2241
Callionymus, 219
Callionymus calcaratus, **2456**
Callionymus goodladi, **2455**
Callionymus japonicus, **1330**
Callionymus richardsoni, **486**
Calliurichthys japonicus (See *Callionymus japonicus*)
Callogobius mucosus, **2476**
Callogobius snelliusi, **2477**
Callogobius sp., **2476**
Calloplesiops altivelis, 156, **244, 1253,** 2224
Calotomus japonicus, **995**
Calotomus spinidens, **631**
Cantherhines, 1905
Cantherhines dumerili, **1348**
Cantherhines fronticinctus, **822**
Cantherhines howensis, **1907**
Cantherhines pardalis, **1354, 1355,** **2493**
Cantherhines sandwichensis (See *C. pardalis*)
Canthidermis maculatus, **120, 1348**

Canthigaster, 823, 1903
Canthigaster bennetti, **402, 826, 827,** **1360, 1635**
Canthigaster compressus, **1638**
Canthigaster coronatus, **1359, 2500**
Canthigaster jactator, **402**
Canthigaster janthinopterus, **823, 1361,** **1634**
Canthigaster margaritatus, **110-111**
Canthigaster punctatissima, **2180, 2181**
Canthigaster rivulatus, **98**
Canthigaster solandri, **98, 402**
Canthigaster valentini, **401, 825, 1358,** **1359, 1902**
CANTHIGASTERIDAE, 96, 823
Caprodon schlegeli, **496**
CARACANTHIDAE, 641
Caracanthus maculatus, **641**
CARANGIDAE, 423, 2227
Carangoides (See *Caranx*)
Caranx armatus, **1055**
Caranx bucculentus, **1054, 2335**
Caranx caballus, **1996**
Caranx caninus, **1996**
Caranx emburyi, **1807**
Caranx equula, **431**
Caranx ferdau, **431, 1809**
Caranx fulvoguttatus, **1808**
Caranx helvolus (See *Uraspis helvola*)
Caranx ignobilis, **1806**
Caranx malabaricus, **1053,** 2227
Caranx mate, 423
Caranx melampygus, **1808**
Caranx sexfasciatus, **1996**
Caranx sp., **1055, 1806, 2335**
CARAPIDAE, 510, 2218
Carapus sp., **510**
CARCHARHINIDAE, 1087
Carcharhinus amblyrhynchos, **2213**
Carcharhinus amboinensis, **2251**
Carcharhinus brachyurus, **2213**
Carcharhinus brevipinna, **2213**
Carcharhinus leucas, **2213**
Carcharhinus melanopterus, **2213**
Carcharhinus obscurus, **2213**
Carcharhinus plumbeus, **2213**
Carcharodon carcharias, 1088, 2211, **2212**
Cardinalfishes, 241, 678, 1433, 1681, **1684,** 2225
Catsharks, 501, 1399, 1666, 2211
Careproctus ovigerum, 2165
Caulolatilus princeps, **1995**
Cebidichthys violaceus, **2102**
CENTRISCIDAE, 319
Centriscus, 319
Centroberyx lineatus, 2219, **2273**
CENTROLOPHIDAE, 1220
Centrolophus, 1220
Centrolophus petersi, **1171**
Centropogon australis, **1823, 2292**
CENTROPOMIDAE, 2223
Centropomus nigrescens, **1972**
Centropyge, 7, 15, 781, 787, 2233
Centropyge acanthops, **780,** 787
Centropyge bicolor, **26, 1133, 1540,**

1541
Centropyge bispinosus, **27, 365, 781,** **1133**
Centropyge eibli, 2233, **2370**
Centropyge ferrugatus, **1, 20, 21,** 21, **1129, 1130**
Centropyge fisheri, **365**
Centropyge flavissimus, 8, **20, 363,** **1543,** 1607
Centropyge heraldi, 8, **18, 19, 1131,** 1607
Centropyge interruptus, **37**
Centropyge loriculus, **22-3, 24**
Centropyge multifasciatus, **1542**
Centropyge multispinis, **782**
Centropyge nox, **362, 1134**
Centropyge potteri, **363**
Centropyge tibicen, **25, 363, 1134,** **1135, 2233**
Centropyge vroliki, **20, 85, 365, 1132,** **1542,** 1607
Centropyge sp., (See *Centropyge interruptus*)
Cephalopholis, 252, 643
Cephalopholis analis, **1484, 1486**
Cephalopholis argus, **499, 642, 1237**
Cephalopholis aurantius, **1238**
Cephalopholis boenak, **492, 644, 1236**
Cephalopholis coatesi (See *Cephalopholis sexmaculatus*)
Cephalopholis leopardus, **652, 1486**
Cephalopholis miniatus, **491, 492, 1485,** **1487, 1839, 1844, 1845, 1854-55**
Cephalopholis pachycentron, **1489, 1851**
Cephalopholis rogaa (See *Aethaloperca rogaa*)
Cephalopholis sexmaculatus, **1483**
Cephalopholis urodelus, **500, 1239,** **1485, 1842**
Cephalopholis sp., **2300**
Cephaloscyllium ventriosum, **1937, 1938**
Cepola, 931
Cepola australis, **1888**
CEPOLIDAE, 931, 1888
Cetorhinus maximus, **1936**
Cetoscarus bicolor, **154, 458, 984, 985,** **1586**
Chaenogobius urotaenia, **478**
CHAENOPSIDAE, 2078
Chaenopsis alepidota, **2085**
Chaetoderma, 1905
Chaetoderma pencilligera (See *Chaetodermis spinosissimus*)
Chaetodermis spinosissimus, **398, 1352,** **1358,** 1905
Chaetodipterus, 1139
Chaetodipterus zonatus, 2014, **2014,** **2015**
Chaetodon, 761
Chaetodon adiergastos, **57, 1191,** 2233
Chaetodon argentatus, **65, 1194**
Chaetodon assarius, 2232, **2365**
Chaetodon aureofasciatus, **1774, 1779,** **1780**
Chaetodon aureus (See *Chaetodon auripes*)

Diademichthys, 1009
Diademichthys lineatus, **1590,** 2217
Dicotylichthys myersi, **1904**
Dictyosoma burgeri, **170**
Dinematichthys, 997
Dinematichthys dasyrhynchus, **2268**
Dinematichthys iluocoeteoides, **996,** 997, **1605**
Diodon, 96, 2246
Diodon holacanthus, **103**
Diodon hystrix, 96, **410, 411**
Diodon nicthemerus, 2246, **2502**
DIODONTIDAE, 96, 2182, 2246
Diplectrum pacificum, **1974**
Diplobatis ommata, **1944**
Diplogrammus, 219
Diplogrammus xenicus, **2455, 2456**
Diploprion bifasciatum, 252, 489, **492, 1228, 1229, 1836, 1837**
Diproctacanthus xanthurus, **447**
Dipulus caecus, 2218
Dischistodus fasciatus, **2377**
Dischistodus melanotus, **1557, 1722**
Dischistodus prosopotaenia, **1723**
Dischistodus pseudochrysopoecilus, **1722, 1723**
Ditrema temmincki, 335, **336, 337**
Doderleina berycoides, **1230**
Dolphins, 1261
Dorosoma petenense, **1951**
Doryrhamphus excisus, **325,** 1420, 1969, **1970, 1994**
Doryrhamphus janssi, **213,** 2220, **2277**
Doryrhamphus japonicus, **213**
Dotalabrus aurantiacus, **2390**
Dotalabrus sp., **2393**
Dottybacks, 156, 2224
Draculo, 219
Dragonets, 219, 2241
Drepane, 1141
Drepane longimana, **1140**
Drepane punctata, **1141, 2231, 2362**
Drums, 1319
Dunckerocampus, 1420
Dunckerocampus caulleryi, 1420
Dunckerocampus dactyliophorus, **325, 1420, 1421**

E
Eagle rays, 1074, 1672
ECHENEIDAE, 1803
Echeneis naucrates, **1803, 1804**
Echidna, 1403
Echidna nebulosa, **353, 1002,** 1403, 2214, **2255**
Echidna zebra, **354,** 1403
Ecsenius, 636, 2239
Ecsenius bicolor, 2239, **2431**
Ecsenius collettei, **1597**
Ecsenius lineatus, **1336,** 2239, **2430**
Ecsenius namiyei, **1592**
Ecsenius oculus, **2432**
Ecsenius pulcher, **470**
Ecsenius yaeyamaensis, **1596, 1597, 2430**
Ecsenius sp., **1596**

Eel blennies, 2240
Eels, 1945, 2214
Ekemblemaria myersi, **2084**
ELASMOBRANCHII, 1934, 2211
Electric rays, 1067
Electric stargazers, 2076
Elegatis bipinnulatus, **1056**
ELEOTRIDAE, 633
Eleotriodes, 633
Eleotriodes elapoides, **175, 474**
Eleotriodes longipinnis, **1894**
Eleotriodes strigatus, **474, 476, 632, 633, 1016, 1603**
Eleotriodes virgatus, **171**
Eleotris fuscus, **1598**
Eleotris oxycephala, **1598**
Eleutherochir, 219
Eleutheronema tetradactylum, **1175**
Ellerkeldia, 2224
Ellerkeldia rubra, 2224, **2307**
Ellerkeldia wilsoni, 2224, **2307**
ELOPIDAE, 1041
Elops machnata, **1042**
Embiotoca jacksoni, 2031, **2033, 2034**
Embiotoca lateralis, **2032**
EMBIOTOCIDAE, 335, 2029
Emblemaria hypacanthus, **2087**
Emblemaria walkeri, **2086**
Emperor bream, 663, 1880
ENGRAULIDAE, 1951, 2215
Engraulis japonica, **1045**
Engraulis mordax, 1951, **1952**
Enneanectes sexmaculatus, **2096**
Enophrys bison, 2159, **2160**
ENOPLOSIDAE, 2233
Enoplosus armatus, 2233, **2370**
Entomacrodus, 636, 2239
Entomacrodus decussatus, **2432**
Entomacrodus striatus, **2433**
Eopsetta grigorjewi, **276, 542**
EPHIPPIDAE, 78, 1138, 2015, 2231
Ephippinae, 1138, 1139
Ephippus, 1139
Ephippus orbis, **1139**
Epibulus, 1729
Epibulus insidiator, **441, 887, 1576, 1577**
Epinephelides armatus, 2224, **2306**
Epinephelus, 252, 643, 1839
Epinephelus acanthistius, **1981**
Epinephelus akaara, **1242**
Epinephelus amblycephalus, **1246**
Epinephelus analogus, **1981**
Epinephelus awoara, **1240**
Epinephelus caeruleopunctatus, **497, 1237, 1246, 1247**
Epinephelus cometae, **261, 1243**
Epinephelus corallicola, **2301**
Epinephelus coromandelicus, **250, 253**
Epinephelus damelii, 252
Epinephelus dermatolepis, **1975, 1976, 1977**
Epinephelus diacanthus, **254, 1240, 1241**
Epinephelus epistictus, **1243**
Epinephelus fario, **645,** 1242, 1249,

1251
Epinephelus fasciatus, **643, 500, 1238, 1239, 1250, 1490, 1853**
Epinephelus flavocaeruleus, **494, 1852**
Epinephelus fuscoguttatus, **1852**
Epinephelus hexagonatus, **493, 1248**
Epinephelus hoedti, **261**
Epinephelus itajara, **1977**
Epinephelus labriformis, **1978**
Epinephelus macrospilus, **1247**
Epinephelus maculatus, **254, 1488, 2301**
Epinephelus megachir, **1249, 1250, 1849, 1850**
Epinephelus merra, **261, 493, 645, 1244, 1491,** 1839, **1847, 1848**
Epinephelus moara, 252, **255, 1242**
Epinephelus multiguttatus, **1979**
Epinephelus multinotatus, **2302**
Epinephelus niveatus, **1981**
Epinephelus panamensis, **1980**
Epinephelus rhyncholepis, **1241**
Epinephelus rivulatus, **2300**
Epinephelus septemfasciatus, **498, 1243**
Epinephelus summana, **497**
Epinephelus tauvina, **493, 1244, 1245, 1840, 1846, 1847, 1856**
Epinephelus tukula, **1244**
Epinephelus undulostriatus, **1802**
Epinephelus sp., **254**
Eptatretus stouti, **1933**
Eptatretus sp., **1933**
Equetus viola, **2009**
Equula, 1165
Erilepis zonifer, 2148
Erosa, 959
Erosa erosa, 959, **961, 2222**
Escolars, 927
Etelis carbunculus, **1292**
Etrumeus micropus, **1045**
Eubalichthys mosaicus, 2245, **2491**
Eucinostomus argenteus, 2003
Eucinostomus gracilis, **2003,** 2003
Eucrassorhinus ogilbyi (See *Orectolobus ogilbyi*)
Euleptorhamphis viridis, 925
Eupetrichthys angustipes, **2396**
Eupomacentrus (See *Stegastes*)
Euthynnus affinis, **1325, 1327**
Euthynnus pelamis, **1327, 1329**
Euxiphipops, 786
Euxiphipops navarchus, **28, 29, 360, 361, 1534, 2369**
Euxiphipops sexstriatus, **16, 361, 1124, 1794, 1798**
Euxiphipops xanthometopon, **30, 31, 359, 783, 1535, 1539**
Eviota, 2242
Eviota abax, **174**
Eviota infulata, **2463**
Eviota sp., **2461, 2462**
Evistias acutirostris, 1217
Evynnis cardinalis, **1313**
Evynnis japonica, **1313, 1315**
Exallias, 636
Exallias brevis, 636, **640, 2433**

Halichoeres centiquadrus (See *H. hortulanus*)
Halichoeres chierchiae, 2054, **2059**
Halichoeres chrysus, **833**, **1572**
Halichoeres dispilus, 2054, **2058**
Halichoeres hoeveni, **603**
Halichoeres hortulanus, **147**, 454, 455, 601, **604, 605, 606, 607, 907, 908, 909, 1574, 1739**
Halichoeres kawarin (See *H. nebulosus*)
Halichoeres leparensis (See *H. argus*)
Halichoeres margaritaceus, **455, 906, 907**
Halichoeres marginatus, **143, 456, 603, 878, 900, 901, 2411**
Halichoeres melanochir, **602, 910, 2413**
Halichoeres miniatus, **903**
Halichoeres nebulosus, **610, 611, 906, 910, 1575**
Halichoeres nicholsi, 2054, **2060, 2061**
Halichoeres nigrescens, **601, 2412**
Halichoeres notopsis (= *H. marginatus notopsis*)
Halichoeres poecilopterus, **137, 451, 899**
Halichoeres prosopeion, **1430**
Halichoeres scapularis, **454, 608, 609, 905**
Halichoeres semicinctus, 2054, **2063**
Halichoeres trimaculatus, **904, 1738**
Halichoeres zeylonicus, **600, 2410**
Halichoeres sp., **2059**
Halieutaea fumosa, **526**
Halieutaea retifera, 525
Halieutaea stellata, **1092, 1093**
Haliophis guttatus, **638**
Halmablennius lineatus, **1338**
Halophryne diemensis, **1821, 2261**
Hammerhead sharks, 1087
Hapalogenys mucronatus, **1310**
Hapalogenys nigripinnis, **237, 1310**
Hardyheads, 1412, 2218
Harengula koningsbergeri, **1048**
Harengula sp., **1413**
Harpadon microchir, **912**
Harpadon nehereus, 913
Harpadon translucens, **912**, 913
HARPADONTIDAE, 913
Hawkfishes, 155, 660, 1143, 2234
Helcogramma decurrens, 2240, **2445**
Helcogramma sp., **2446**
Helicolenus hilgendorfi, **268**
Helicolenus sp. (See *Sebasticus albofasciatus*)
Helotes, 1887
Helotes sexlineatus, 1887, 2225, **2318**
Hemanthias peruanus, **1988**
Hemigymnus, 577
Hemigymnus fasciatus, **144**, 577, **582**
Hemigymnus melapterus, **145**, 577, **583, 584, 864, 1740**
Hemilepidotus hemilepidotus, 2159, **2161**
Hemipteronotus dea, **132, 450, 866**
Hemipteronotus pavoninus, **2063**
Hemipteronotus pentadactylus, **446, 865**
Hemipteronotus taeniurus, **149, 445, 867, 868, 869, 1568, 2414**
Hemipteronotus verrens, **865**

Hemipteronotus sp., **865**
HEMIRAMPHIDAE, 925, 2218
Hemiramphus commersoni (See *H. far*)
Hemiramphus far, **1415**, 2218, **2270**
Hemiramphus sajori (See *Hyporhamphus sajori*)
Hemiscyllium indicum, 1083
Hemiscyllium ocellatum, **1665**, 1666
Hemiscyllium trispeculare, 1666, 2211, **2249**
Hemitaurichthys polylepis, **41, 1214**
Hemitaurichthys zoster, **768, 769**
Heniochus, 39, 75, 761
Heniochus acuminatus, **38**, 39, **69**, 75, **368, 369**, 761, **1209, 1210, 1756**
Heniochus chrysostomus, **70, 1212, 1213, 1529, 1755, 1756**
Heniochus monoceros, **71, 72, 1210**
Heniochus permutatus (See *H. chrysostomus*)
Heniochus pleurotaenia, 761, **766, 767**
Heniochus singularius, **70, 1210, 1211**
Heniochus varius, **70, 369**, 767, **1206, 1207, 1208, 1754**
Heraldia nocturna, **2280**
Hermosilla azurea, **2012**, 2014
Herrings, 313, 1951
Heteroclinus, 2240
Heteroclinus adelaidae, **2451**
Heteroclinus eckloniae, **2449**
Heteroclinus heptaeolus, **2450**
Heteroclinus roseus, **2450**
Heteroclinus sp., **2452**
Heterocongrinae, 1945
HETERODONTIDAE, 504, 1664
Heterodontus, 1664
Heterodontus francisci, **1935**
Heterodontus galeatus, **1664**
Heterodontus japonicus, **507**
Heterodontus portusjacksoni, 1664, **2249**
Heterodontus zebra, **506, 1085, 1086**
Heterodontus sp., **1935**
Heterostichus rostratus, **2096**
HEXAGRAMMIDAE, 2149
Hexagrammos decagrammus, **2150, 2151, 2151**
Hexagrammos otakii, **540**
Hexagrammos sp., 2149
Himantura, 1673
Hippocampus angustus, 2220, **2281**
Hippocampus breviceps, **2281**
Hippocampus coronatus, **211, 212**
Hippocampus ingens, 1969, **1969**
Hippocampus japonicus, **211**
Hippocampus kuda, **209**, 211, **326**
Hippocampus mohnikei, **210**
Hippocampus spinosissimus, 2220
Hippocampus sp., **214**
Hippoglossus stenolepis, 2175
Hirundichthys oxycephalus, **923**
Histiogamphelus cristatus, **2278**
Histiophryne bougainvilli, **2267**
Histiopterus, 1217
Histiopterus acutirostris, **1216**, 1217
Histiopterus typus, **1216**

Histrio, 259
Histrio histrio, 259, **271, 1366**
Holacanthus, 7
Holacanthus arcuatus (See *Apolemichthys arcuatus*)
Holacanthus clarionensis, **2022, 2023**
Holacanthus passer, **2024, 2025, 2026**
Holacanthus trimaculatus (See *Apolemichthys trimaculatus*)
Holacanthus venustus, **17**
HOLOCENTRIDAE, 230, 689, 1966, 2220
Holocentrinae, 1966
Holocentrus, 230, 689
Hologymnosus annulatus, **592, 875**
Hologymnosus doliatus, **145, 447, 874, 1728**, 1729
Hologymnosus semidiscus (See *H. doliatus*)
Holorhinus tobijei, **1076**
Holotrachys, 689
Hoplolatilus purpureus, **1590**
Hoplopagrus guentheri, **1999**
Hornfishes, 391
Hughichthys, 663
Hyperlophus sp., **1815**
Hyperoglyphe, 1220
Hyperoglyphe japonica, 1220
Hyperprosopon argenteum, 2031, **2034**
Hyperprosopon ellipticum, **2035**
Hypoatherina tsurugae, **316**
Hypodytes longispinis, **517**
Hypodytes rubripinnis, **518, 536**
Hypoplectrodes nigrorubrum, **2308**
Hyporhamphus dussumieri, **2270**
Hyporhamphus melanochir, 2219, **2270**
Hyporhamphus sajori, **331**
Hypseleotris guentheri, **1602**
Hypsoblennius brevipinnis, **2098**
Hypsoblennius gentilis, **2098**
Hypsopsetta guttulata, **2175, 2176**
Hypsurus caryi, 2034, **2035, 2036**
Hypsypops rubicundus, **2051**
Hysterocarpus traski, 2029

I
Ichthyoscopus lebeck, **983**
Icichthys, 1220
Icichthys lockingtoni, 1220
Iniistius dea (See *Hemipteronotus dea*)
Iniistius pavo (See *Hemipteronotus dea*)
Inimicus, 959
Inimicus didactylum (See *Rhinopias argoliba*)
Inimicus japonicus, **515, 536**
Inimicus sinensis, 2296
Ioglossus sp., **2114**
Iso rhothophilus, **2271**
Isobuna, 660
Istiblennius, 636, 2239
Istiblennius chrysospilos, **2434**
Istiblennius coronatus, **471**
Istiblennius edentulus, **1339, 2435**
Istiblennius lineatus, **1338, 2436**
Istiblennius meleagris, **1339, 2436**
Istiblennius periophthalmus, **2437**

Istiblennius sp. (See *Praealticus margaritarius*)
Istigobius hoshinonis, **178**
Istigobius ornatus, **1014, 2475**
Istigobius spence, **2474**
ISTIOPHORIDAE, 1257
Istiophorus platypterus, **1259**
Isurus oxyrinchus, **1937**

J

Jacks, 423, 2227
Jawfishes, 2070, 2238
Jewfishes, 2224
Johnius, 1319
Jordania zanope, 2157, **2158**
Julis musume (See *Coris musume*)

K

Kathetostoma averruncus, **2077**
Kelpfishes, 2235
Kentrocapros aculeatus, **414**
Knifejaws, 543
Kryptophanaron alfredi, 1411
Kuhlia, 308
Kuhlia sandvicensis, 308
Kuhlia taeniura, **236, 308, 791**
KUHLIIDAE, 308
KYPHOSIDAE, 443, 1163, 2014, 2230
Kyphosinae, 2014
Kyphosus, 433, 1163, 2231
Kyphosus analogus, **2013**
Kyphosus cinerascens, **237, 1162, 1163, 1835**
Kyphosus cornelii, 2231, **2359**
Kyphosus elegans, **2013**
Kyphosus gibsoni, **2358**
Kyphosus lembus, **1162**
Kyphosus sydneyanus, **2358, 2359**

L

Labracinus (See *Dampieria*)
Labracinus cyclophthalmus (See *Dampieria cyclophthalmus*)
Labracoglossa argentiventris, **419**
Labrichthys, 587
Labrichthys unilineata, 587, **594, 595, 862**
LABRIDAE, 128, 569, 1729, 2054, 2236
Labrisomus xanti, 2094, **2094**
Labroides, 128, 587, 2236
Labroides bicolor, **136, 593, 861**
Labroides dimidiatus, **129, 136,** 159, **255, 407, 453, 651, 688, 861, 1487, 1545, 1580, 1581, 1687, 1789, 1800, 1839, 1856, 1872, 1875**
Labroides pectoralis, **453**
Labroides phthirophagus, **340**
Labroides sp. cf *phthirophagus* (See *Labroides pectoralis*)
Labropsis alleni, **1581**
Lactophrys, 1899
Lactoria, 1899
Lactoria cornuta, **102, 413, 1364, 2496**

Lactoria diaphanus, **415**
Lactoria fornasina, **103**
Lagocephalus lunaris, **405**
Laiphognathus multimaculatus, **2437**
Lampris regia, **323**
Lancetfishes, 1257
Lantern-eyes, 1411
Lateolabrax japonicus, **336, 1252**
Lates calcarifer, **1235,** 2223, **2298**
Leatherjackets, 1905, 2244
Left-eyed flounders, 262, 2168, 2243
Leiocottus hirundo, **2159**
LEIOGNATHIDAE, 1165
Leiognathus, 1165
Leiognathus dussumieri, **1166**
Leiognathus elongatus, **1166**
Leiognathus equulus, **1164**
Leiognathus nuchilis, **236**
Leiognathus rivulatus, **1164, 1166**
Lepadichthys frenatus, **165**
Lepidoblennius marmoratus, 2240, **2446**
Lepidotrigla microptera, **536, 1007**
Lepidotrigla sp., **1008**
Lepidozygus, 717, 2234
Lepidozygus tapeinosoma, **716, 717**
Lepophidium prorates, **1963**
Leptocephalus, 260
Leptoscarus vaigiensis, **628, 993,** 2238
LEPTOSCOPIDAE, 2239
Leptosynanceia, 959
LETHRINIDAE, 663, 1880, 2227
Lethrinus choerorhynchus, **435**
Lethrinus chrysostomus, **1514, 1880, 1881, 1882**
Lethrinus fletus, **1298, 1299**
Lethrinus harak, **1301**
Lethrinus kallopterus, **1300**
Lethrinus leutjanus, **1300**
Lethrinus mahsenoides, **664**
Lethrinus miniatus, **1297**
Lethrinus nebulosus, 1880, **1881**
Lethrinus reticulatus, **418**
Lethrinus variegatus, **1301, 2345**
Lethrinus xanthocheilus, **1301**
Lienardella fasciata, **450, 451, 879, 1582,** 1729, **1731**
Limanda schrenki, 1097
Limnichthys fasciatus, 2239, **2428**
Liocranium praepositum, **2293**
Lionfishes, 258, 653, 2221
Liopropoma fasciatum, **1984**
Liopropoma lineata, **1481**
Liopropoma susumi, **1481**
Liopropoma sp., **1480, 1481**
Liparid, 168
Liparis pulchellus, 2165, **2167**
Lissocampus runa, **2279**
Liza vaigiensis, 2235, **2388**
Lizardfishes, 335, 2215
Lo, 1753
Lo vulpinus, **92,** 93, **95,** 1753
Loach gobies, 172
Lobotes, 1265
Lobotes pacificus, 1265
Lobotes surinamensis, **1265**
LOBOTIDAE, 1265

LOPHIIDAE, 508
Lophiocharon trisignatus, 2218, **2265**
Lophiomus setigerus, **508, 509**
Lopholatilus chamaeleonticeps, 531
Lophonectes, 262
Lotella, 2218
Lotella fuliginosa, **2267**
Lotella maximowiczi, **170**
Lovamia aroubiensis, **1683**
Lumpsuckers, 2165
LUTJANIDAE, 221, 673, 2227
Lutjanus, 221, 2227
Lutjanus amabilis, **1866**
Lutjanus argentimaculatus, **1280, 1282, 1868-69**
Lutjanus argentiventris, **2000, 2002**
Lutjanus bohar, **672, 1280, 1516, 1865**
Lutjanus carponotatus, **226, 1867, 2338**
Lutjanus chrysotaenia (See *L. carponotatus*)
Lutjanus decussatus, **1281**
Lutjanus erythropterus, **1284, 1285, 1290**
Lutjanus flavipes (See *L. fulvus*)
Lutjanus fulviflamma, **226, 673, 1282, 1287, 1288, 1289, 1864, 2339**
Lutjanus fulvus, **1278, 1283**
Lutjanus gibbus, **672, 1277, 1515, 1518**
Lutjanus janthinuropterus (See *L. fulvus* and *L. lemniscatus*)
Lutjanus johni (See *L. fulviflamma* and *L. russelli*)
Lutjanus kasmira, 221, **227, 1279, 1516, 1863**
Lutjanus lemniscatus, **1285, 2339, 2340**
Lutjanus lineolatus, **1288**
Lutjanus lutjanus, **1288**
Lutjanus nematophorus, 221
Lutjanus peru, **2000**
Lutjanus quinquelineatus (See *L. spilurus*)
Lutjanus rivulatus (See *L. bohar* and *L.* sp.)
Lutjanus russelli, **226, 1276, 1865**
Lutjanus sebae, 221, 673, **674, 1518, 1870, 1871**
Lutjanus semicinctus, **1281**
Lutjanus spilurus, **1278, 1517, 1868**
Lutjanus superbus, **1286**
Lutjanus vaigiensis (See *L. argentimaculatus*)
Lutjanus viridis, **2002**
Lutjanus vitta, **436, 1289**
Lutjanus sp., **1280**
Lycodes pacificus, **1964**
Lythrypnus dalli, 2105, **2111**
Lythrypnus pulchellus, **2110**

M

Mackerels, 1325
Macolor niger, **349,** 673, **674, 1276**
Macolor sp., **1519**
Macropharyngodon bipartitus, **624**
Macropharyngodon meleagris, **456, 876, 877**